The Smuggling Coast

'*Watch the wall, my darling, while the Gentlemen go by . . .* '

Riding his pony along the Solway shore some 50 years ago, the young John Thomson, now a prominent Dumfries businessman, heard the old fishermen tell tales of days gone by when punitive Excise duties made the local populace turn to smuggling. Now he has gathered these and other stories from the heyday of 'the free trade' to make a fascinating account of the smugglers' wiles and the efforts of the revenue officers to outwit them.

'*Brandy for the Parson, baccy for the Clerk . . .* ' Yes, and tea for the Minister's wife, laces for the Laird's lady, salt for adding savour to folk's dishes—tragic and comic are the stories, from the young Manxman shot dead on the eve of his wedding while evading the revenue cutters to the canny toll-keeper, spotting the Customs man leading away a seized horse and cart with contraband kegs, who followed behind in the darkness and stealthily removed keg after keg to hide them by the wayside. And through it all the dogged pursuit by the brave officers of the Customs and Excise, on sea and by land, facing danger from the elements as well as from their quarry.

Robert Burns, the famous Dumfriesshire poet, was an Exciseman; Sir Walter Scott, the nineteenth-century novelist, a regular correspondent of one of the Collectors of Customs, wrote about the smugglers and their tricks in many books. The testimony of these and other men of letters is woven through the fabric of the plain accounts from the Customs books to form a rich tapestry of the time when the Solway Scots pitted their wits against the grasping English taxman.

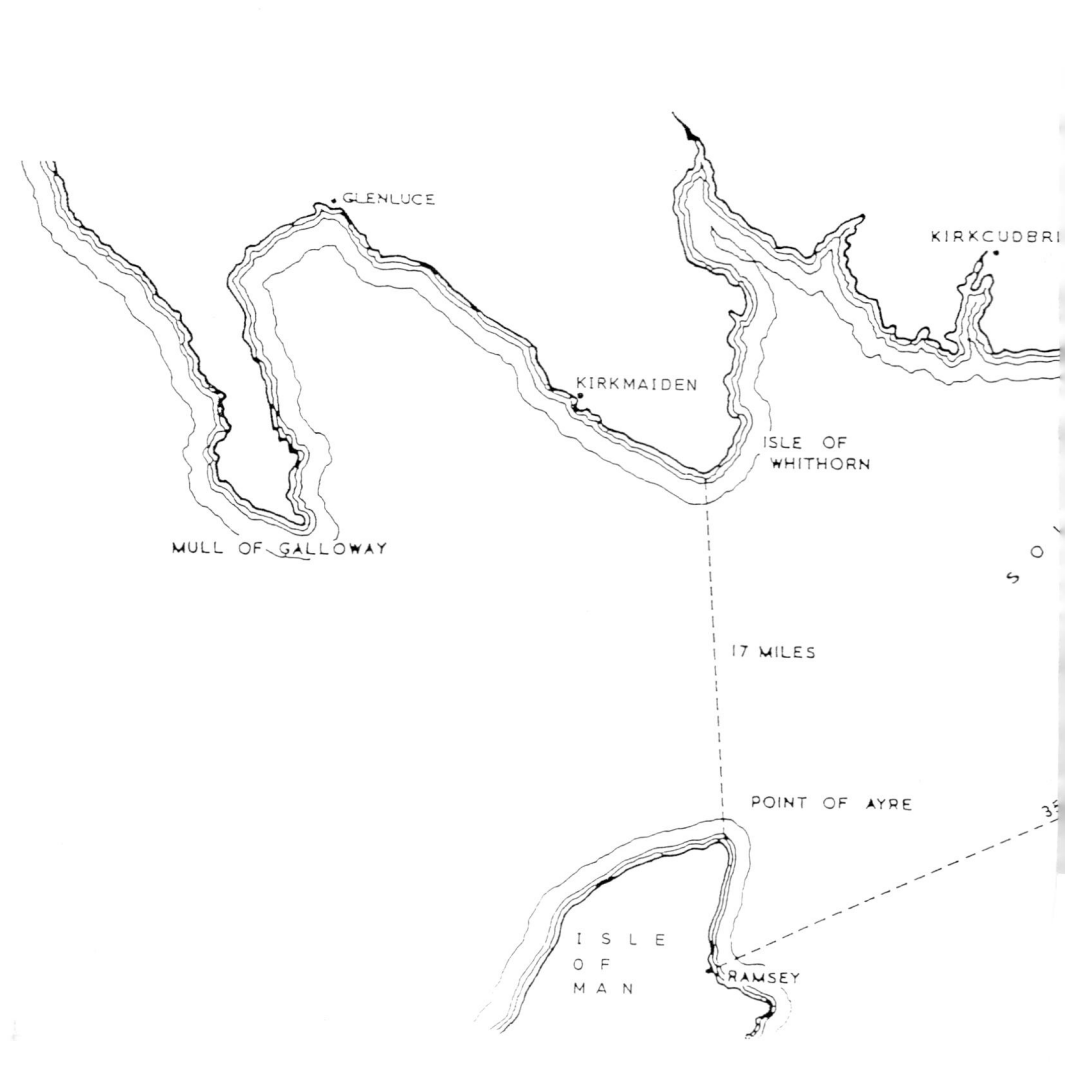

GLENLUCE

KIRKCUDBRI

KIRKMAIDEN

ISLE OF
WHITHORN

MULL OF GALLOWAY

S
O

17 MILES

POINT OF AYRE

3

I S L E
O F
M A N

RAMSEY

'Encounter at Sea' by Michael Barton

THE SMUGGLING COAST

The Customs port of Dumfries
Forty miles of the Solway Firth

by

JOHN A. THOMSON

Published by
T. C. FARRIES & Co Ltd
Dumfries

First published 1989 by T. C. Farries and Co Ltd, Irongray Road, Lochside,
Dumfries DG2 0LH, Scotland, UK.

ISBN 0 948278 14 5

Typeset in 10 point Garamond from an Amstrad PCW

Printed in Great Britain by Headley Brothers Ltd The Invicta Press Ashford Kent
and London

Acknowledgements

I have received help from so many people but in particular I am indebted to the following for their kind permission to use material from their records.

The Keeper of Records in Edinburgh. Most of the unattributed quotations are from the original letter books of the Customs service held by the Scottish Record Office in Charlotte Square.

The Archivist of HM Customs and Excise.

The Curator of Whitehaven Museum.

The Librarian of the Ewart Library, Dumfries.

And all their staff members who helped so willingly.

Without the enthusiastic research of my son John and the typing of my daughter Patricia this book would never have been completed.

ERRATA
Painting by Clarkson Stanfield
ANNAN WATERFOOT
Courtesy of Aberdeen Art Gallery & Museum
Aberdeen City Arts Department
Page 4 – Charles I in 1644 not 1664
Page 97 1833 should read 1883

A Smuggler's Song

If you wake at midnight, and hear a horse's feet,
Don't go drawing back the blind, or looking in the street,
Them that asks no questions isn't told a lie.
Watch the wall, my darling, while the Gentlemen go by!
Five and twenty ponies,
Trotting through the dark—
Brandy for the Parson,
'Baccy for the Clerk;
Laces for a lady, letters for a spy,
And watch the wall, my darling, while the Gentlemen go by.

Running round the woodlump if you chance to find
Little barrels, roped and tarred, all full of brandy-wine,
Don't you shout to come and look, nor use 'em for your play.
Put the brishwood back again—and they'll be gone next day!

If you see the the stable-door setting open wide;
If you see a tired horse lying down inside;
If your mother mends a coat cut about and tore;
If the lining's wet and warm—don't you ask no more!

If you meet King George's men, dressed in blue and red,
You be careful what you say, and mindful what is said.
If they call you 'pretty maid,' and chuck you 'neath the chin,
Don't you tell where no-one is, nor yet where no one's been!

Knocks and footsteps round the house—whistles after dark—
You've no call for running out till the house-dogs bark.
Trusty's here, and *Pincher's* here, and see how dumb they lie—
They don't fret to follow when the Gentlemen go by!

If you do as you've been told, 'likely there's a chance,
You'll be give a dainty doll, all the way from France,
With a cap of Valenciennes, and a velvet hood—
A present from the Gentlemen, along o' being good!
Five and twenty ponies,
Trotting through the dark—
Brandy for the Parson,
'Baccy for the Clerk.
Them that asks no questions isn't told a lie—
Watch the wall, my darling, while the Gentlemen go by!

RUDYARD KIPLING

Contents

List of illustrations   x
Prologue   1
Early days   4
The Customs port of Dumfries from
  the Sark to the Urr   8
The Customs men and the ships they
  sailed   13
Free trade and foul play   18
Over the seas from Man   24
Human cargoes   32
Annan smugglers   37
As others saw us   43
The stormy sea   48
The Collector writes   51
The Salt Duties   55
Lingtowmen and others   61
Fifty years on   64
The bumper years   69
The ebb and flow of the smuggling tide   73
Robert Burns, Exciseman and poet   77
Smuggling between Scotland and England   83
Returning to honest ways   91
Epilogue   98

Appendix 1: Dumfries establishment:
  Collectors of Customs   99
Appendix 2: Eighteenth-century duties
  and returns for 1796   100

List of illustrations

Map of the Solway Firth   iii
Encounter at sea, by Michael Barton   frontispiece and cover
Solway shipping, by James Mitchell of Maryport   7
Customs' oath of allegiance   15
The grave of François Thurot   27
Safely landed, by Michael Barton   31
Annan Waterfoot, by Clarkson Stanfield   41
Out of sight, by Michael Barton   53
High and dry, by Michael Barton   67
Letter from Robert Burns   81
Hoisting sail off Carsethorn, by Michael Barton   96
Dumfries Establishment 1870   97

The watercolours reproduced in this book are by Michael Barton, a marine artist who spent some time on the Solway coast. He illustrated Ronald T. Gibbons' book To the King's Deceit, *published by Whitehaven Museum. 'Annan Waterfoot' was painted by Clarkson Stanfield RA in 1841, when he visited Annan at the end of his tour of Scotland. His illustrations appear in an early edition of Scott's* Waverley Novels. *This picture is reproduced by kind permission of Aberdeen Art Gallery. James Mitchell of Maryport, whose oil painting of Solway shipping appears on page 7, attracted considerable attention at the turn of the century.*

Prologue

This is a story of the Customs and Excise services and of the smugglers who have tried over the years to outwit them. Until as recently as 1909 the two were separate—often competing—organisations. The officers of the Customs dealt with imports of goods from abroad—wine, spirits, tea, coffee, tobacco, silks—and those of the Excise watched over home-produced goods—whisky, beer, salt, candles. The Excisemen were also responsible for the collection of the many different duties imposed by successive governments to raise money—hearth tax, window tax, entertainment tax and, in our own time, value added tax. I am assured by a friend in the enforcement service that VAT avoidance is still considered fair game by some . . .

My interest in the smuggling legends was first stirred as a child. I was brought up on a farm stretching from the two busy Annan railway stations down to the Solway shore and, with a succession of sure-footed—if sometimes unreliable—ponies I could explore every little nook of the coast from Powfoot to Redkirk. At that time—50 years ago—there were far more people on the shore, shore-walkers and fishermen, and seats positioned at the foot of each of the loanings going down to the edge of the sea. In good weather the seats were always occupied by old men with exciting tales to tell—and only one generation further back their grandfathers had been involved, or had known somebody who was involved, in the daring smuggling days.

One old man, in the traditional fisherman's blue jersey, I remember particularly: he told me that on his father's eighth birthday the first steamship came up the River Annan to the harbour and because it happened on his birthday his father had never forgotten it. The sailing packets from Liverpool were assisted by steam engines from about 1826, when the Carlisle and Liverpool Steam Company was in business; by 1834 they had competition in the form of the Carlisle and Annan Steam Navigation Company and protection in the form of the first steam Customs cutter, the *Vulcan*. All these vessels, however, still had auxiliary sails.

Later my interest was sharpened by reading the many tales of smuggling, from Robert Burns to Graham Smith, the librarian and archivist of HM Customs and Excise, so now I thought that I would

1

draw together the many strands before the stories of a great-grandfather were entirely forgotten.

To every tale there is a beginning and an end. So I decided to keep
this one within the boundary of the jurisdiction of the Customs Port
of Dumfries—from the River Urr at Dalbeattie to the head of the Solway at Gretna. If there seems to be undue emphasis on Annan, this is
because the town features extensively in the district smuggling
annals—possibly because Annan (certainly a smuggling hotbed) was
at least considered worthy of intensive policing by the Revenue
Service whereas, in the Kirkcudbrightshire end of the district, the
officers' efforts were much restricted by the difficult coastline and
terrain. Annan is also, of course, my home town, and my grandfather
was once its Provost.

A book such as this is bound to be based on the work of others and
I cannot claim much originality for it. The reports of a succession of
parliamentary committees have provided many original opinions
and, by great good fortune, the *Letter Books of the Customs Port of
Dumfries* are among the most complete in the country and go back to
1708.

The dangerous fast flowing tides of the Solway are today almost
entirely empty of shipping so it is difficult to imagine smuggling
boats entering the Firth unseen, but in former years there was a veri-
table confusion of traffic to conceal the smugglers' passage. From
1650 shipping in the Solway multiplied at a tremendous rate until by
1790 there were almost 500 trading vessels belonging to the ports of
the Cumberland Solway coast alone. These averaged about 150 tons
burden, with crews of 5 to 20 men, and were a major source of
employment.

Hutchinson's *History of Cumberland*, published in 1794,
describes how an average ship would cost £2,000 to fit completely;
and that 90 ships belonging to the Cumbrian Solway port of Maryport ranged from 50 to 250 tons, an average of 150 tons. Each was
crewed by some seven men and a boy, all keen to supplement their
wages if the risks were not too great.

Tobacco came from America, timber from the Baltic, and coals
went to all parts of the world. most of the Maryport coal went to
Ireland, although many of the smaller ships took cargoes to Scottish
harbours. Whitehaven was then the third largest port on the Western

shores of Britain. In the Scottish harbours trade was much quieter than on the English coast and the ships considerably smaller, probably only carrying 30 to 50 tons of goods and crewed by two men and a boy. However, almost 100 sloops, schooners and wherries, a few larger brigs and barques, and large numbers of fishing boats were registered on the Dumfriesshire and Kirkcudbrightshire coasts, all constantly coming and going with the tides on their lawful and partly lawful occasions in the trade of the Solway.

Smuggling, however, was never deemed to be a serious crime by the people of Scotland, who indeed delighted in the widespread belief that it deprived the English of the proceeds of unpopular taxes. All classes, therefore, could enjoy the luxuries provided by the smugglers with a clear conscience.

Early days

When smuggling is spoken of today we immediately think of international airports or drug runners sailing into small harbours in the Mediterranean—or, more recently, converted Scottish fishing boats carrying cannabis into Cornish coves or lonely Argyll harbours. But only 200 years ago so many people in Dumfriesshire and Kirkcudbrightshire were actively engaged in the trade that it was second only to farming as a money earner in the district. Smuggling was not a great problem in the old kingdom of Scotland because Customs duties were never very great. It was in any case not regarded too seriously.

Stealing of livestock or 'border reiving' took up most of the Warden's time in this part of Scotland's border with England. Only in the reign of James I of Scotland (1424–36) did a 'plain account' appear, dealing with the exports of wool and skins and laying down a duty of 12 pence (Scots) in the pound sterling on the value of cattle, sheep and horses exported.

Later revenue laws were aimed at restricting English trade and confining foreign traffic to the Scottish Royal Burghs—of which Dumfries and Annan were two. In the seventeenth century, after the 1603 Union of the Crowns, there were many Customs decrees. Among them was one forbidding the sale of imported English ale (far superior to the Scottish brew) in 1625.

In 1643 the Solemn League and Covenant was signed, exhorting both Scottish and English parliaments to establish Presbyterianism in defiance of Charles II. As General Leslie led the Scots parliamentarian army south to support their fellows in the English Civil Wars, the Marquis of Montrose was travelling north, to Dumfries, to raise a Scottish army for the king. On 15 April 1664 Montrose left his foot soldiers and baggage at Annan while he galloped on to occupy Dumfries before the parliamentary army arrived.

Needing a large sum of money quickly the Scots parliament passed the first-ever Scottish Excise Act. This imposed a duty of 2s 8d per Scots pint on whisky (a Scots pint was the equivalent of three modern English pints; Scots usually drank by the mutchkin, ie one-quarter of a Scottish pint, while stronger men ordered a Chopin of ale—or two mutchkins)!

From this small beginning Scotland's national drink has, over the centuries, produced prodigious sums of money for successive Chancellors of the Exchequer.

From that first Act, one of the earliest references to smuggling in our area concerns the notorious Jabobite Sir Robert Grierson, who persecuted the Covenanters and was responsible for many 'Martyrs of the Covenant'. As a reward for this evil work, possibly, Grierson was one of three partners successful, in 1684, in obtaining His Majesty's Customs and Excise when they were rouped by the Scottish Exchequer for £28,000 yearly.

A document in the public records in the Register House, Edinburgh, dated 1 April 1684, entitled 'A bond anent Irish victual for the Lairds of Lag and Kelburn' details the undertaking of Robert Grierson and John Boyle of Kelburn, by order of the Privy Council, 'to search for, seize and apprehend all Irish victuall and cattle, and salt beef made thereof, as shall be imported from Ireland into any harbour, river, etc . . . to burn any boats or vessels . . . secure the persons of the Skippers'; they bind themselves that in carrying out these instructions they will not sell any of the 'victual.' for their own advantage.

These instructions were afterwards embodied in an Act of James VII of Scotland (James II of England) in 1685.

After the unsuccessful Jacobite rising of 1715 both Sir Robert and his son William appear to have become themselves involved in smuggling. Indeed, at their house of Rockhall, near Collin, it was reputed that there were two beacons to enable smuggling boats away out in the Firth beyond and below to fix their position.

In this, as in other illegal projects, they employed the Jacobite exiles among their continental agents. One of these, Patrick Gordon, wrote from Bordeaux in 1735 to express regret that so much of the cargo had been lost—and this letter, as was usual, came by smuggling vessels via the Isle of Man.

In 1689 when William and Mary succeeded James II of England Customs and Excise duties in Scotland were increased to pay for the Dutch Wars. These duties were small and simple matters compared to the English Customs and Excise system.*

---

*Before the Union of the Parliaments a computation of the relative wealth of England and Scotland produced a ratio reflected in Customs and Excise revenue of 36 to 1—such was the lack of trade in Scotland. (*Scottish History Society*, Ed T.C.Smout, Vol 1978 p 9.

The English coinage, weights and measures, in all their complexity, were also applied to Scotland after the Union of the Parliaments in 1707, when a separate Scottish Board of Customs was set up under the Act of Union. It was unified with the English Board 15 years later but this did not produce the successful results prophesied by London; and the Scottish Board, under its own Lords Commissioner, was re-established in 1742.

The ingenious, persistent smugglers of the Solway continued to bring in grain and cattle from Ireland until 1707, when they turned their attention to more profitable, less bulky, cargoes. In 1695 David Crawford of Dumfries was empowered by the Scottish government to seize grain from Ireland and confiscate the boats; however, it was then discovered that having taken bribes from the smugglers he had granted them licences to carry on their trade!

It might seem that heavy duties on goods would only encourage evasion but there was then no other way of raising income for the government. Money was a rarity, most wealth being held either in property or in goods. The landed classes paid tax on their property, but the only way to catch the mercantile classes was to levy a tax on their goods at some controllable point—such as the two routes between Scotland and England, or at the harbour of a Royal Burgh.

As duties on imports increased and gradually reached the same level as existed in England, smuggling became an important part of the economy of the Solway coast. The duty increases ranged from two to seven times the old Scottish rates although some things, such as salt, attracted less duty in Scotland than in England. The Scottish courts were fairly lenient towards smugglers—free traders—and eventually this led to English enforcement officers being brought over the border to control the coast, the jurisdiction of the Customs Port of Dumfries being extended along the Scottish coast from Dalbeattie to the border with England at Gretna. The western end of this area was officially described as 'Cummertrees, Annan and the Entry of Sark'. The 'Entry' seems to have started near Battlehill, a mile west of Annan Waterfoot, which had been of great importance as it led to the flourishing harbour of Redkirk town; but a gigantic storm, in 1670, caused the Solway to wash away much of Redkirk village, including the church. The site, however, continued to be a landing place for several generations of smugglers sending goods into England—to such effect that in 1698 the first Riding Officers employed in the north of England were to patrol the Scottish border. The men in Whitehall must have been out of touch with reality, as they considered a surveyor and three riders to be adequate—although they were allowed firearms for self-defence!

'Solway shipping', by James Mitchell of Maryport

The Customs Port of Dumfries from the Sark to the Urr

Smuggling was almost universal in Scotland, for the people, unaccustomed to imposts, and regarding them as an unjust aggression upon their ancient liberties, made no scruple to elude them whenever it was possible to do so.

SIR WALTER SCOTT (1771–1832) *Heart of Midlothian*

There is a marked contrast between the Dumfriesshire and Kirkcudbrightshire coasts. Dumfriesshire is fairly level, with a sandy shore, easier to keep under observation and easier to ride from one part to another if an unknown boat were sighted; whereas Kirkcudbrightshire has a rocky shore with over 30 secluded bays and coves between Southerness and Fleet—ideal for secret landings of contraband and unseen departures of pack horses laden with goods, which could move quickly into the hills where the Excisemen dared not follow. Even given no time to move the cargo, the coast of Kirkcudbrightshire is studded with caves and natural hiding places. It also has many little islands, or at least rocky outcrops, behind which many a boat may be concealed from the main Solway channel, while the Dumfriesshire shore has very few.

The *Statistical Account* of 1790 recorded that the Solway Firth was navigable at high water for vessels of 100 tons burden as far as seven or eight miles east of Annan, and that vessels could lie in safety anywhere along the shore, all of which was flat and mainly sandy. The inhabitants of Annan itself, however, owned only five sloops and two ferry boats plying to and from the Cumberland coast.

Often the sandy Dumfriesshire shores showed clearly the marks of men, boats and carts unloading cargoes, yet the enforcement officers could do little; for the local populace was wont to mob them, even to hold them prisoner for a day or so, until the smuggled goods had disappeared into the well-planned system, which often included gypsies as carriers and landed gentry as protectors.

The smugglers of the Solway were not as savage as those of Kent and Sussex, where fatal battles with the preventive men were often recorded as regular events. On the Solway shore women often proved themselves as violent as the men and most houses had a hiding place of some kind which was protected by the womenfolk. Several houses had secret entries below the fireplace, with a good fire always burning in the grate when revenue officers approached. Often pigs lay on top of the contraband cellar. On a larger scale, whole coastal farms could command large rents from smuggling syndicates.

Even the Church sometimes joined in—in the manse at Colvend there was a large cellar with a concealed entry. And some smugglers preferred supernatural protection: I remember my grandfather's tale that under one flat gravestone beside Annan town hall there was no body, but a wood-lined grave for the safe storage of spirits.

However, the smugglers were not always able to hide. In 1733 Captain Roper's sloop seized the Annan boat *Prosperity* and took her into Whitehaven on the English coast—together with her cargo of brandy from the Isle of Man. According to her log she had been sailing coastwise from Liverpool to Annan with a legitimate cargo.

At this time the Customs men got almost half the value of the contraband they seized as prize money; thus the loss of such a substantial reward for the Scottish Customs was a serious matter. Often there were disputes between the English and Scottish authorities when vessels were seized in the Solway, with the Navy appearing to prefer the safe port of Whitehaven. The Scottish Board in Edinburgh, in an attempt to calm its staff, wrote: 'The manner in which the Port of Dumfries is laid out is such that it is uncertain how far its authority extends into the Firth'.

The following Commission (reproduced by kind permission of Whitehaven Museum) gave authority to an English Customs cutter to seize goods in the Scotish part of the Solway.

'We the Commissioners for Managing and causing to be levied and collected His Majesty's Customs, Subsidies and other Duties in that part of Great Britain called Scotland, and also the duties of Excise upon all Salt and Rock Salt Imported or to be Imported into that part of Great Britain called Scotland, do hereby Depute and Impower

Joseph Bell, Mate of the *Lynx* cruizing vessel in the service of the Revenue in England

to be an officer of the Customs to Seize uncustomed and prohibited goods, by virtue whereof he hath Power to Enter into any Ship, Bottom, Boat or other vessel, and also at all Lawful Times to Enter into any House, Shop, Cellar, Warehouse or other Place whatsoever; there to make diligent Search into any trunk, Chest, Case, Pack, Truss, or any other Parcel or Package whatsoever for any goods, Wares or Merchandize Prohibited to be exported or Imported, or whereof the Customs or other duties have not been duely paid, and the same to Seize to His Majesty's use, and to put and Secure the same in the Warehouse of the Port next the Place of Seizure: in all which premises he is to proceed in such manner as the Law Directs, Hereby Praying and requiring all and every His Majesty's Officers and Ministers and all others whom it may concern to be aiding and assisting to him in all things ás becometh, GIVEN under our Hands and Seal at the Custom-house in EDINBURGH the Eleventh day of February in the Eighteenth year of the Reign of OUR SOVEREIGN LORD KING GEORGE the Third and in the Year of Our Lord one Thousand seven Hundred and seventy eight.'

This Commission was signed by no less a person than Adam Smith, author of *The Wealth of Nations*, who had been appointed a Commissioner of HM Customs in 1778. The other two signatories were George Cl (possibly Clark) Maxwell and 'Cochrane', who could have been Basil Cochrane.

On the Nith there were harbours not only at Dumfries but also at Glencaple, Kelton, Kingholm and Dumfries Dock (the latter is now known as Dock Park). On the west bank were Lagghall, Kirkconnel, New Abbey and, at the mouth of the river, Carsethorn. This complex owned 40 coasting vessels and two or three larger boats employed in the Baltic trade. Carsethorn was traditionally the most important for vessels from Dumfries which, when meeting with a south westerly wind, anchored in the bay until they had a fair wind to carry them past the Solway sandbanks. Vessels for Dumfries took on a pilot and tide waiter, cleared quarantine and waited for high tide. Liverpool and Irish packet boats called at Carsethorn: it is reported that travellers complained that even the best inn there was poor and dirty, with little comfort, but that the welcome was always cheerful.

The importance of Carsethorn as a trading harbour declined after 1747 when Glencaple was developed; but it continued to be the centre from which the overworked Customs men carried out another of their many government duties, enforcing quarantine regulations for vessels from abroad. With no cures then for many of the diseases brought back from foreign parts the Customs men took the precaution of putting a Bible in a box at the end of a long pole—the idea being that the ship's captain could swear that his crew had no fever, before the Customs officers stepped aboard.

The Customs boat at Carsethorn was always busy, yet when in 1768 it was in urgent need of repair (at a cost of about £3) Edinburgh prevaricated. The expenditure was finally approved, but when a bill arrived for £4 11s a full explanation was demanded by the chief book keeper in Edinburgh who failed to appreciate the dangers faced by the crew of a boat constantly in action, although they were well reported. One such story, of February 1778, tells us that while the boat was out on patrol it was attacked by no fewer than three smuggling vessels at the Water of Urr and its crew suffered injuries requiring the attention of Mr Ferguson, Surgeon—whose fee was three guineas.

Unlike most ports, Dumfries had no fine, permanent Customs headquarters. One reason was that larger vessels involved in foreign trade were only able to come upriver as far as Carsethorn (where remarkably little remains of the landing places) or, later, to Glencaple. Another was the lack of legitimate trade, making the main importance of Dumfries its use as a preventative force headquarters against smuggling. Throughout much of the eighteenth century the annual legitimate foreign trade consisted only of four or five tobacco ships from Virginia, two or three carrying timber from the Baltic and a few with cargoes of wine from Oporto and Bordeaux.

At the height of the Isle of Man free trade the mass of goods in transit ensured that one large legitimate business prospered: that was the building of boats. Larger yards, capable of launching vessels of 20 tons or more, seemed to be established on the Scottish side of the upper Solway at Annan, Glencaple, Kelton of Dumfries and Rockcliffe, near Dalbeattie (this latter village a possible source of confusion for smugglers and Customs authorities alike, for there was a Rockcliffe at each end of the coast patrolled by the Dumfries Customs cutters!)

The Lords Commissioner of Customs in Edinburgh considered that in Dumfries a room for an office and a cellar in the collector's private house were all that was warranted, from 1707 to 1798. Then a building was rented in Shakespeare Street, possibly to be shared with the Excise men, for 30 guineas per annum—considered to be a great improvement; in 1760 the collector had complained that 'we have neither chairs nor desks worth anything'. A large street plan produced by one John Wood of Dumfries in 1819 showed the Shakespeare Street Customs House, opposite the Theatre Royal, but in 1832 it was on the move when premises were rented in Bank Street. The Excise office in Dumfries also moved several times; after 1800 it was in Nith Place and it is now in the High Street.

The new Customs house contained a long room, collector's office, comptroller's office, four rooms for books and papers, a warehouse and cellar room and a kitchen and bathroom for the housekeeper as well. The landlady, Mrs Harriet Pew, received a rent of £35 per annum on condition that she kept the building wind- and water-tight. The Customs were to pay, each year, £1 10s for police tax, 6s 8d for road money and 15s for the poor assessment.

The 'long room' may in fact have been square or even round, but it was so called because after 1671 all public rooms in Customs houses were called long rooms; in that year a new Customs house had been built in London, with a great long room running the whole length of the river front for all import and export business transactions.

It is interesting to note that at Kirkcudbright, for a rent of £10 pa, there was a long room with adjoining closet for the tide waiter and a separate room as a warehouse. In Annan an allowance of £5 pa was paid for the use of one room in the dwelling house of the coast officer, plus a cellar to hold the beam and weights. At Barlochan, on the River Urr, and at Carsethorn a yearly allowance of £2 was made to the boat captains for the use of a store in their own houses.

The Customs men and the ships they sailed

I must down to the seas again, for the call of the running tide
Is a wild call and a clear call that may not be denied.
JOHN MASEFIELD (1878–1967), *Sea Fever*

From the description of the area covered by the Customs Port of Dumfries it might be imagined that a staff of at least 100 stout men would be required; but the government in London in its wisdom decided that 15 were quite sufficient—that was in 1710. By 1717 it was increased to 21. These were:

Title	Salary pa
Collector	£50
Deputy Collector	£25
Comptroller	£40
Deputy Comptroller	£20
Land Surveyor	£40
Land Waiter and Searcher	£25
Overseer of boatmen	£30
10 Tidesmen or Tide Watchers/Waiters	£15
4 Boatmen	£15
yearly total	£440

A Customs man was hedged in by a great many regulations and instructions. He had 'to seek diligently for any false bulk-heads or private places' where goods might be concealed. He was forbidden to invite his wife or friends on board and he was forbidden to accept any treat or entertainment from the master or mate of the ship; and any candle he took below decks had to be secured in a lantern.

The lowest grade, and that in which most were employed, was that of tide waiter or tide watcher, paid at £15 pa. Their duty was to watch for ships coming in with the tide and to inspect them as they dropped anchor. Later regulations said that each ship should be boarded by two tide watchers—to prevent the single man being bribed or intoxicated by the ship's captain. Tide waiters were forbidden to act as merchants, brokers or innkeepers; and strictly forbidden to attend any political meetings or to interfere in the election of a Member of Parliament.

A letter, dated 1727, from the collector describes his disposition of tidesmen: 'John Johnstone at Riggheads [6 miles east of Annan]; John Shand at Annan; William Edwards at Annan; Adam Colquhoun at Dumfries; Thomas Bain at Dumfries; Robert Stewart at New Abbey [6 miles from Dumfries]; Robert Loughton at Carsethorn [10 miles from Dumfries]; James Affleck at the mouth of the River Urr [8 miles from Carsethorn] and Alexander Campbell at Auchencairn [3 miles from the Water of Urr].' He concludes by saying that 'some of these would require more officers to guard the coast and particularly between this town and the English Border'. The Ruthwell tidesman, one of the 10 allowed on the Dumfries establishment, is missing from the collector's list.

A tidesman had to be vouched for by two securities and, like everyone else in the Customs service, take an oath before a Justice of the Peace. (This is reproduced on the facing page.)

One Robert Neilson took the oath at Annan in 1741 and, resisting the many bribes he was offered, continued as tidesman for almost 30 years. His record tells us that he had a wife and three children, whom he kept on £15 a year. Customs men, however, received a small pension on retirement. The widow of a Carsethorn boatmen who died in the execution of his duty received an annuity of £10 from the Board of Customs and a small pension must have been a necessity—a reasonably conscientious Customs man could not expect any favours in his old age! Every year a few officers received testimonials; one of the Dumfries men thus recognised was F. P. Lewis, who in 1873 was given a purse of 25 sovereigns.

After 1700 the vessels carrying most of the free trade in the upper Solway were either small handy sailing boats, known as 'scouts', or large, heavily armed luggers, mounting as many as 22 guns and with a crew of up to 50 men. However, there were still a few dependent on oars alone, which gave a great advantage in shallow waters.

With the Union of the Parliaments in 1707 the first Customs enforcement cutter was sent to Scottish waters to patrol the Solway coast and prevent the Isle of Man trade. These became known as the 'preventive cutters', remembered for the length of their bowsprits and the great size of their jib sails. Almost invariably single masted, they were rigged fore and aft with a bowsprit that could be run out. They were clinker built and broad in the beam and required a fairly large crew to sail and fight them. It must be said that the hazards of

You are to bear in mind the solemn Declaration which you have taken on your admission into office, viz.—

I_____

solemnly and sincerely declare, that I will be true and faithful in the execution, to the best of my knowledge and power, of the Trust committed to my charge and inspection in the Service of Her Majesty's Customs, and that I will not require, take, or receive, any Fee, Perquisite, Gratuity or Reward, whether Pecuniary, or of any sort or description whatever, either directly or indirectly, for any Service, Act, Duty, Matter, or Thing Done or performed, or to be done or performed, in the execution or discharge of any of the Duties of my Office or Employment, or any account whatever, other than my Salary, and what is or shall be allowed me by Law, or by any special Order of the Lords Commissioners of Her Majesty's Treasurty, or the Commissioners of Her Majesty's Customs for the time being.

the sea caused greater losses among revenue cutters than did the smugglers. Between December 1819 and October 1822 five boats, the *Speedwell*, *Vigilant*, *Hardwick*, *Sprightly* and *Ranger* were lost by shipwreck as far apart as Portland Bill in Dorset and Fraserburgh in the north, with the loss of many lives.

Identifying the activities of individual revenue cutters is not easy because the prudent support given by the Scottish Commissioners to the reigning Royal Family by naming their boats after them meant that there were no fewer than three *Royal George*s and three *Prince of Wales*es at different times; and small boats often had names similar to those of the larger vessels.

The revenue ships, seven of which had been built for the Scottish Commissioners around 1725, lacked the speed and manoeuvrability of many of the craft used by smugglers. The end of the century, however, saw many improved ships in service and in 1774 four fast cutters owned by the revenue service are recorded in the Solway area:

- the *Royal George*, built in 1778 of 141 tons and 64 feet in length, armed with 10 carronades, 2 long nine-pounders and 2 long six-pound guns, crewed by 60 men;
- the *Royal Charlotte*, of 66 tons, with a large crew of 60 for shore landings;
- the *Prince of Wales*, built in 1777 of 155 tons, with a wide beam of 23 feet 6 inches, and 16 guns, crewed by 52 men;
- the *Princess Elizabeth*, with a 50-man crew.

There were also seven sloops and small cutters:

- the *Royal George*;
- the *Prince of Wales*, built in 1793 of 60 tons with 8 three-pounder guns, crewed by 32 men;
- the *William Henry*;
- the *Princess Royal*;
- the *Prince Edward*;
- the *Prince Ernest Augustus*;
- the *Osnaburgh*.

To add to the confusion there was also a wherry of 36 tons called the *Prince of Wales*—its principle duty was to prevent salt smuggling from Ireland to Scotland.

The cutters varied greatly in size. The following table, extracted from the archives of the Customs service shows regulation dimensions laid down by one controller.

Tonnage	Length	Beam	Draught	Mast Height	Mast iameter
150 tons	72ft	22ft 10ins	10ft	75ft	21ins
100 tons	62ft	20ft	9ft 6ins	68ft	17ins
60 tons	54ft	16ft 8ins	9ft	56ft	14ins
50 tons	50ft	15ft 9ins	8ft 6ins	55ft	13ins

And very item was costed right down to a spy-glass at £7 6s 0d.

As late as 1840 south west Scotland still had four revenue cutters, mainly engaged in the prevention of smuggling between Scotland and Ireland:

• at Ayr, the *Vulcan*, one of their earliest steamers, with a crew of 31;

• at Stranraer, the *Wellington*, of 36 tons, built in 1815 with 8 guns and a crew of 34, which spent much of its service at Stranraer until it was struck off in 1842.

• at Port Patrick, the *Harriet*, crewed by 14 men;

• at Luce Bay, the *Ferret*, of some 39 tons and 7 crew members.

The commissioners of Customs did not use local shipbuilders, but the first *Statistical Account of Scotland* mentions that an Excise cutter of 60 tons was being built in Kirkcudbright in 1794.

The cutters' crews were armed with cutlasses, those stout naval swords as handy for cutting loose the rigging as for cutting down a foe; and the appearance of any one of the Customs cutters would strike anger in the hearts of men aboard a smuggling boat thinking themselves set fair for a welcoming lantern in a friendly cove. Those waiting on the shore would be forced to run for cover and many are the tales of chases, near misses and occasional captures which kept up the spirits of the Customs men on the bleak waters of the Solway— and filled the pages of this book.

Free trade and foul play

He either fears his fate too much,
Or his deserts are small,
That puts it not unto the touch
To win or lose it all.
MARQUIS OF MONTROSE (1612–1650), *My dear and only Love*

This sums up the philosophy of several generations of Solway smugglers and their trading partners. The Solway was only a port of entry and goods had to be moved not only north and south but also east, up Eskdale and Liddesdale and Ewes, then down the valley of the Teviot—some 70 miles—to Yetholm, which was a great distribution centre for Berwickshire and Northumberland. The wealthy, the wise and the witty members of society then found their claret even more enjoyable if it had avoided Customs duty, just as many pillars of society do today when returning from foreign travel with extra bottles or tobacco.

It is recorded that half the inhabitants of the two villages of Yetholm were engaged in smuggling. Kirk Yetholm (known as 'the gateway to England') had been from time immemorial the headquarters of the Scottish gypsies under the leadership of the Faw family. Old Will Faw, the first gypsy king, was buried there in 1784 and his descendants were also taken there for interment. Gypsies were often called Egyptians at that time (the name 'gypsy' comes from 'Egyptian' because they were thought to have originated in Egypt) and in 1711 the Justices of the Peace for Lanarkshire reported that large numbers of Egyptians were gathered together in companies and 'are passing through the country armed with swords, guns, pistols and durks, especially in the mountainous places of the shires of Tweedale, Nithsdale and the Stewartry of Annandale where they commit many crimes'. After 1855, when the cross-border smuggling of whisky came to an end, the gypsy population left this little border village.

In the years following the Union of the Parliaments in 1707 there were probably several hundred small-scale, legal brewers connected with inns or provision stores in Dumfries and Galloway, as well as a score of larger breweries. These kept the Excise officers busy, resulting in occasional neglect of the smugglers who brought, at a reasonable price and at considerable personal risk, those comforts which, when duty had been paid to the government, were too expensive to buy. But the Customs strength was not increased until 1710, possibly as a result of a petition which showed the indignation of the legal traders:

'Petition of the Merchant Traders within the Town of Dumfries To the Lord President at Edinburgh on 5th July 1709

'Humbly showeth that it is well known to this honourable Convention that it is the privilege of the Royal Burghs only, to import merchandise and other staple commodities from the Plantations and other places beyond the seas for which privilege the Royal Burghs are assessed and taxed in the sixth part of tax of the whole Kingdom of which sixth part your Petitioners do pay a part, conforming to what your Honours have taxed the town of Dumfries at. But considering that the small trade which we formerly had is now wholly monopolised by setts, partnerships and clubs of gentlemen Freeholders and others within this country, and further who these several months byegone has driven (extended) the whole trade of this country further than any merchants used to do, by their importing great and considerable quantities of Brandy and Tobacco, which they have run and carried ashore in several bye creeks, such as in the Water of Sark, Cummertrees and others. And have stocked not only all this country but likewise Teviotdale, the Merse, Cumberland and Northumberland on the English side. And have had a ship of considerable burden lying off and cruising along the coast full of Brandy and Tobacco which is run and carried out in several places; and which offered to sink the Queen's boat and any other boats except those of her own friends, that offered to come near her. And particularly upon Thursday being the last of June last, there was 24 packs of tobacco seized in Annandale by William Johnstone of Bearholm Collector of Her Majesties Customs here, and brought back within a mile of this place, but the same being owned by a person who is known not to be worth a groat, he applied, as we are informed, to some Justices of the Peace and showed them a sham transfer from Robert Douglas Collector of Customs at Glasgow, albeit it can be proved that the said tobacco was lifted at a place to which it had been embezzled and carried from the sea. Upon which the said Justices did give him a Warrant to recover and carry the said tobacco. Which by collusion, it seems the Collector yielded unto. And it is said that a certain gentleman concerned both in the smuggling trade and in the Collection [of Excise] at Glasgow did immediately destroy the said pretended transfer, thinking the foresaid warrant to be sufficient. And we further represent that there was a loading of Brandy about the month of April last found in some waste houses at Newby, which was seized by the said Collector. And having sent a part of it up to Dumfries he secured, as he thought, the rest within the town of Annan— but upon the first Sabbath Day in the morning after the seizure, a great number of men with drawn swords and pistols cocked entered the town on horseback and broke up the houses where the Brandy was lodged and employed all the wheel-carts in the town of Annan to carry off the same, besides the carts they brought with them. And in open daylight they are known to unload boats and carry off the goods both in the English and Scots side to a considerable quantity which, as has been informed by all, has come from the Isle of Man.

'And albeit that we have several times laid the same before the Officers of the Custom House here, yet we have found no effectual redress, but the aforesaid incroachments still increase and grow worse and worse . . . '

The attack in Annan on the Sabbath probably took place while the Reverend Thomas Howie kept the inhabitants—Customs men included—in church with a lengthy sermon—perhaps on the text 'Render unto Caesar that which is Caesar's', the sort of preaching which went unheeded by his smuggling parishioners!

Gaining access to the cellars of Annan merchants was, it seems, more difficult than breaking into the Customs store; as Mr Short, the collector, found in 1710 when he hired a gig to take him to Annan to review the tobacco stock of a Mr Black. Probably he was the only person to be surprised that Black had gone abroad and that his men had no authority either to let the collector see or weigh the tobacco. Ten years later the collector went with several assistants and refused to be put off so easily. Both merchants whom he wanted to see on that later occasion about two landings of brandy at Annan were away, and had taken the cellar keys with them; but he broke into the cellars to find that in both the brandy stocks differed by such a huge amount from the records that he had to write to his superiors in Edinburgh to ask for instructions.

In the burgh of Dumfries duties on alcohol were a particularly bitter bone of contention as it was one of the few towns in Scotland empowered by parliament to levy a local tax. When it was introduced in 1716, the 91 brewers and retailers in Dumfries had to pay two pennies (old Scots money) on every pint of ale or beer sold within the burgh. Although collecting this was not one of the Customs men's tasks, its unpopularity rubbed off on them. Another great annoyance both to honest traders and to the revenue men was the number of peclars or packmen who travelled the country districts with bladders of spirits and plugs of tobacco bought cheaply from smugglers to supply the needs of farmers and farm workers farther inland.

The Solway shore at the height of the smugglers' activity bore no small resemblance to Chicago in the Prohibition years. Gangs of lawbreakers were prevalent and for many years Customs warehouses were regularly broken into by marauding parties and the contents carried off. Towards the close of 1711, one gang assaulted the officer in charge of Kirkcudbright and rifled his premises; another, at about the same time, got into the warehouse at Dumfries with false keys and carried off five cwt of tobacco. Some years later a crowd of smugglers and their friends mobbed the magistrates and collector at Dumfries to win back four casks of confiscated brandy that had been forwarded from Annan for safe storage.

This report of a similar incident was sent to Edinburgh by the collector on 2 May 1726:

'This is to inform you that upon 28th ult. the King's warehouse here was broken open betwixt one and two of the clock that morning, and five casks of brandy taken out thereof; to our great surprise, considering the strength of the warehouse, for it had a strong double door, with a big lock and padlock affixed by a chain, which everybody thought impregnable; but it appears the door has been forced open by a crow iron and the great chain broken by the same instrument. As soon as we were informed of the same we immediately got a warrant to search for the stolen brandy, and were informed that it was lodged in the Bridgend Dumfries, where we found it in a house belonging to Robert Newall, Wright there, and brought the same back to the warehouse.'

It is then stated by the writer that, after great exertion, two of the 'authors of the villainy' had been apprehended and that he expected all the others would be secured. For once a happy ending for the Customs men!

A Mr Briceson, who was both a merchant in Leith and a Solway smuggler, was also brought to the attention of the Lords Commissioner:

'A Leith merchant, named Briceson, is described as "one of the greatest contraband runners upon the coast", for the apprehension of whom both the Excise and Customs Officers held warrants, which they had vainly tried to enforce. It was his practice, to run tobacco and brandy from the Isle of Man to the Solway coast, sell as much of them as he could to the people of the district and then send the rest overland to his establishment at Leith.

'On the 12th August, 1726, while a Revenue boatman named Affleck [presumably James Affleck—see page 14] was proceeding to Dumfries with three casks of brandy which he had seized at Glenluffen Moss, Briceson appeared upon the scene. He had brought the liquor across the sea to a friend; and not liking the idea of its being diverted into another channel, he, assisted by the son of his confederate, set ruthlessly upon the Revenue Officer, who had to relinquish his prize. He was glad to escape from the smugglers with his life.'

The Customs men had also to contend with the country squires, as Robert Stewart, a riding waiter, found to his annoyance in 1711 when he watched an Isle of Man boat from 11 o'clock in the morning to 11 o'clock at night when it landed—at the Wherry Creek only half a mile from Arbigland House. Three horses and two servants belonging to Adam Craik of Arbigland arrived at 4 am and conveyed 120 gallons of brandy to the 'Big House'—where Stewart dared not touch it. It is interesting to note that a few years later the gardener at this same Arbigland House was the father of the famous privateer, Paul Jones.

One of the strangest tales (recorded in the *First Statistical Account of Dumfries*) from the days when Dumfries carried on 'the honourable trade' concerns an English gentleman who took advantage of the Union of England and Scotland to travel to Dumfries where he knew he could buy large quantities of tobacco at an attractive price. He carried gold, enabling him to settle without any paper records. He placed his purchases in a reputable merchant's warehouse and promised to arrange transport whenever the weather improved. No message ever came and no trace was ever found of him. The town council finally obtained approval from the High Court to sell the cargo; and the money was used to rebuild the road from Dumfries to Annan.

Every three or four years in the course of the eighteenth century parliament appointed yet another committee to consider the legislation made to prevent the running or smuggling of goods; and always they proposed yet more Bills to provide what they hopefully called 'more effective detection of such fraudulent practices'. Needless to say much of this parliamentary labour was in vain due to the difficulties of enforcement and the high rewards of evasion; both accentuated in this area by the proximity of the Isle of Man.

Over the seas from Man

Now the great winds shoreward blow.
Now the salt tides seaward flow;
Now the wild white horses play,
Champ and chafe and toss in the spray.
MATTHEW ARNOLD (1822–1888), *The Forsaken Merman*

In some parts of Scotland the rule of law prevailed; but not on the Solway coast, only 25–30 miles from the Isle of Man, then a small independent state with contraband running as its main industry. Joseph Train's *History of the Isle of Man* tells us that it was a comparatively poor fishing community until after 1700 when a large company of adventurers from Liverpool settled at Douglas to carry on a contraband trade with the surrounding shores. The island became a great storehouse whither the French and the Dutch sent vast quantities of goods which were carried off by the smugglers in barques, boats and wherries into Scotland, England, Wales and Ireland 'to the detriment of the King's revenue and prejudice of the fair trader'. It was very large-scale smuggling. One seizure, at Annan in 1720, netted four big casks of brandy and 12 hogsheads of wine.

It was always apparent to the authorities that the export of prohibited articles, as well as the import of contraband goods, was on the increase and therefore a reform of the protective system on the Solway was urgently needed. To achieve this, representatives from the ports of Dumfries, Whitehaven, Carslisle and Workington held a conference at Wigton in Cumberland on 20 November 1724; they agreed to lay before the Customs authorities certain remedial proposals.

They recommended that two well armed and well manned sloops should be procured, fitted both for sailing and rowing, and that one should be stationed at Silloth, on the English side, with the other at Annan Waterfoot. The latter would command the open channel, while the smaller boats in service would be deployed along the shore.

The Dumfries collector, in urging adoption of this scheme, advised:

'The charge of each of these sloops would amount in the first year to £180 and afterwards to £130 yearly, which indeed will be an additional charge upon the revenue; but I am convinced your Honours will find it very sufficiently made up, either by the increase of the King's share of seizures, or the advance of the duty collected at the foresaid ports, and particularly the duty on tobacco, for not withstanding the great quantity of tobacco made use of in this country, there is but a small consumption of what is legally imported and fairly pays duty, which makes it plain that there are vast quantities of this commodity run from the Isle of Man.'

In a vain attempt to regain control in the Solway the Customs service accepted the report and ordered two fast sailing skiffs resembling the shape of an Isle of Man boat, each 20 feet long and costing £12, with full outrig, to be built at Whitehaven. They were stationed on each side of the Firth, the passage between them being so narrow that it must have been difficult for any boat to pass undetected; though at the same time little revenue yawls would still be needed to cruise among the sandbanks and up the creeks after any contraband-carrying craft successful in eluding these two guardians of the channel.

In 1742 Thomas Wilson, Bishop of Man, wrote: 'Our people are mightily intent upon enlarging the harbours at Peel, Ramsay and Douglas; but the iniquitous trade carried on, to the injury and damage of the Crown, will hinder the blessing of God from falling upon us.'

The Bishop was also critical of the Lord of the Isle who, deriving advantage from 'a small duty on exports and imports paid to him and providing an average annual surplus of £7,293 for the ten years 1755–1764, a very large income at that time'. Among the lord's other prerogatives he laid claim to 'all waifs and strays'. It was not surprising that he ignored the Bishop, who warned that a commerce founded on trick and fraud could not be followed without an entire surrender of principle. But the good Bishop had little effect and the Duke of Atholl—who by marriage into the Stanley family had acquired the island from the Earl of Derby in 1739—continued to support the Manx laws which discouraged outsiders as on the one hand a stranger was exposed to imprisonment and sequestration of their property for the smallest debt while on the other Manxmen were protected from incarceration for the largest.

In time of war, smuggling skills could be turned to other uses as

François Thurot, one of the most famous Manx smugglers, discovered. He rose to command the French naval squadron of three ships, which in February 1760 in the course of the Seven Years' War forced Carrickfergus Castle to surrender.

The Collector of Customs was a man of importance in Dumfries; and when news of Thurot's war activities reached the Provost he immediately sent for David Blair, the collector, to discuss how best to deal with this threat. the town was in a state of excitement and there was much speculation about the fate of vessels out in the Solway. Collector Blair ordered a 24-hour watch by all his staff, keeping messengers ready to carry any news back to the Provost. He also dispatched a well-mounted courier with an urgent report to the Lords Commissioner in Edinburgh.

When news of the enemy ships reached Commodore Elliot, the British commander, he set sail from Kinsale, in Ireland, with three navy vessels; a week later he came face to face with Thurot, north of the Point of Ayre, the northern tip of the Isle of Man. At the ensuing battle, in Luce Bay, Thurot's flagship the *Belle Ile* (of 44 guns) was sunk, 300 French sailors died and 1,200 were landed as prisoners in Ireland. Thurot himself—who was only 33—was killed; he is buried in the kirkyard of Kirkmaiden, which nestles by the shore near Glasserton.

This letter, dated 1762, from the Dumfries Customs office to their superiors in Edinburgh (initialled by David Blair the collector and James Ewart the comptroller), gives an accurate description of the small Manx smuggling vessels and what they could carry, as well as describing their crews and means of sail or rowing and, finally, how they were condemned and cut up with saws and hatchets.

'8th February 1762

'Sirs,

'We are directed by your letter of the 4th February to acquaint your Honours with the size or tonnage and condition of each of the seven Manx Boats returned for Condemnation in our letter of 1st February.

'We beg leave to acquaint your Honours that the above mentioned boats are all open, about five or six tons burden and generally bring from the Isle of Man, betwixt forty or fifty small casks of spirits, containing about eight or nine gallons

The grave of François Thurot, Kirmaiden kirkyard

each, or six or eight hundred weight of tea in leather bags in each boat. They are rigged sometimes, with two masts and two square sails and at other times only one mast and one sail and for calm weather they row with four oars, and carry eight men in each boat.

'We further beg leave to acquaint your Honours that the hulls of these boats were cut to pieces with saws and hatchets to prevent the manx men and smugglers from carrying them off. And since part of them is carried off by the County people for firewood and the remains carried off by the flood so that in effect they are totally destroyed.

'There was an absolute secrecy for this procedure—the boats being seized at different parts on the firth and at a considerable distance from Dumfries The rigging and furniture of the five boats seized by the Late Mr Blair, are at Annan, twelve miles from Dumfries and the rigging of the two seized by the Collector and William Main the Land Waiter are at Glencaple four miles distant from Dumfries as it would have cost a considerable sum to have carried them there. We are of the opinion that the furniture of the forementioned boats would sell to greater advantage if your Honours would give directions to have them condemned before the Justices of the Peace and sold there.

'D. B.   J. B.'

To encourage Manxmen to earn an honest living by fishing the government charged no duty after 1772 on salt—used to cure fish—sent to the Isle of Man. However, the Manx found it more profitable—and easier than fishing—to smuggle the salt back into Britain, evading duty and selling it at a profit. Less adventurous Manx boats lay offshore and intercepted trading and fishing vessels which purchased small quantities of contraband goods and brought them ashore concealed in their legitimate cargoes. The small force of revenue men had neither time nor inclination to search all these local boats.

Port O'Warren, a famous name in the annals of smuggling, is a small cove that until 1970 could only be reached, other than from the sea, by a precipitous flight of steps. Of all the tales told of that lonely spot none is more poignant than that of the young Manxman who, on the eve of his wedding and anxious to earn some money, tried to run a small cargo of salt into this bay, accompanied only by his future brother-in-law. They were challenged by the revenue cutter *Ernest Augustus*, commanded by Sir John Reid. The young bridegroom failed to stop— whether from fright or because he knew no English is not known—a shot was fired and he fell, fatally wounded. The other young man beached the boat and fled, eventually returning to Ramsey to tell the sad story. The body of the bridegroom was laid to rest in Colvend churchyard by sympathetic villagers but the grief of his family was so great that they, including the bride, got permission to come to Colvend, remove the body and sail back home with it. Unfortunately on the return journey a squall blew up, the ship capsized and they were all drowned.

This terrible tragedy aroused so much indignation that Sir John Reid was charged with murder, a most unusual event in smuggling history. Not surprisingly, though, he was acquitted.

During the eighteenth century smuggling in the Isle of Man had increased so much that the annual returns of trade were said to be at least £350,000 while the value of Excise seizures was not more than £10,000, showing enormous profits for those engaged in the illegal trade. In 1765 the sovereign rights of the Duke of Atholl as Lord of the Isle of Man were purchased by the British Crown for £70,000, in an effort to control the island and particularly to prevent its use as a smuggling base. Great abuses continued, however, and enforcement officers were appointed from those formerly active in the illicit trade. New regulations were brought in, that all goods had to be imported from England only and landed nowhere other than Douglas, with a maximum fixed quantity; and none of this might be carried in ships of less than 70 tons—the idea being to prevent the use of all the other small harbours round the island's coast. These regulations, however, had less effect than expected by the government in London which knew little of the courage and skill of the smugglers.

It is interesting to note that John Paul Jones, born at Arbigland, near Carsethorn, was the first shipmaster listed in the Douglas *Customs Book* to bring licensed goods from England to the Isle of Man after it was annexed to the British Crown and after these new regulations came into force.

It is not surprising that a seaman of such enterprise, who had learned his skills among the local smugglers, went on to help found the American Navy. In 1773 he left the smuggling waters of the Solway—but not for good. In 1775, at the start of the War of American Independence, he joined the American Navy and was given command of the *Ranger*, a 26-gun frigate. In April 1778 he sailed from the French port of Brest and on 15 April seized the *Lord Chatham*, a ship bound from London to Dublin, putting a crew on board to take her back to France. Two days later he sank a Scottish coasting schooner loaded with barley.

The following day, two miles north of the Isle of Man, the *Ranger* was spotted by Captain Gurley, commanding the small armed Customs cutter *Hussar*. Undaunted by the size of the unknown ship, Captain Gurley hailed her to ascertain her business; for reply the gun ports were knocked open, the decks filled with men and every gun that could be brought to bear fired upon the *Hussar*. The little Customs ship tacked several times, keeping as much as possible on the ship's quarter, until, with sails and rigging badly damaged, she got out of reach of the guns of John Paul Jones.

That gentleman's most daring exploit came on 22 April when he landed and burned some ships in the busy, fortified harbour of Whitehaven. Then he sailed over to observe the county of his birth and made an unwelcome call on the Earl of Selkirk at St Mary's Isle, Kircudbright, where he helped himself to the silver plate and other valuables. A message was immediately sent to Dumfries requesting help to repel the three-masted American privateer. The Customs supervisor there expected him to come to Carsethorn, near Arbigland, but discretion prevailed and John Paul Jones left the Solway, never to return.

After leaving St Mary's Isle he stood out for the Irish Channel, where a fishing boat told him that the British naval sloop *Drake*, of 20 guns, was pursuing him from the north. Immediately he altered course towards her and reported that: 'On 24 April I took His Majesty's sloop *Drake* with 157 officers and men after a hard fought battle of one hour four minutes pure and simple broadsiding at close range. The result of the action was due entirely to the superior gunnery of my crew.'

Few adventurers have captured even one king's ship, but only an outstanding seaman of great courage could capture a second; this John Paul Jones did in September 1779 when HMS *Serapis*, of 44 guns, surrendered after five hours of bloody battle off Flamborough Head.

A few years later, after the end of the War of American Independence, he entered the service of Russia. In 1787 Marshall Prince Potemkin sent Paul Jones to oversee the fitting-out of the Russian Black Sea fleet, and in June he led it out to defeat the Turkish fleet at the Battle of the Liman; for this victory the Empress Catherine rewarded him with the Order of St Anne. In 1788 he became a Rear Admiral in the Russian Navy.

Mr Truckle, formerly Curator of Dumfries Museum, found another little-known connection between John Paul Jones and the Solway in this extract from the *Annandale Observer* of 9 November 1979:

'Paul Jones, it appears, was not married but had an "affaire

'Safely landed', by Michael Barton

d'amour" with a Madame Theresa Townsend, and in the *Dum-fries Standard* of 7th July, 1844, an obituary notice recorded—"At Watch Hill by Annan, on 8th inst. at an advanced age William Paul, son of the celebrated Captain Paul Jones, died".'

From a Solway seaman to an American naval captain and then to a Russian Rear Admiral—indeed a remarkable achievement for a boy brought up among the smugglers of the Solway Firth!

Human Cargoes

In the seventeenth and eighteenth centuries smuggling was not confined to goods. People too were often carried. Jacobites were taken to the Isle of Man and thence to France and Rome, and lesser men who were skilled workers were also carried, for it was an offence to entice artisans to go abroad, punishable by a fine not exceeding £100 and by three months' imprisonment—penalties which were increased later, in the reign of George II. The Customs men had to act as policemen in those days and the prevention of secret comings and goings was a part of the lives of all ranks of the service.

The Maxwell family, whose lands extended from the borders of Ruthwell to the Nith and beyond, were staunch supporters of the Catholic faith and devoted to the cause of the Stuart kings. As a result the Caerlaverock shore was used as a safe point for the illegal entry of Catholic priests and Jacobite agents. Many of the family suffered for their faith, among the first of whom was Robert, Earl of Nithsdale, who during the Civil War after defending Caerlaverock Castle for 13 weeks in 1640, had to surrender to the king's enemies. After five years of war he was smuggled to the Isle of Man where he died in 1646.

One of the last of the family to suffer was William, Earl of Nithsdale, whose wife Winifred provides one of the most romantic tales of history. After the Jacobite rising of 1715 William was captured, sentenced to death and imprisoned in the Tower of London, from which there was usually no escape. When Winifred heard the news she set off from Dumfries, with only two servants, to ride through the harrowing winter weather to London. Once there, she discovered that the king would show no mercy so, after much preparation and with the help of her maid, one dark night after visiting her husband in the Tower she led him out, dressed as her maid, and with a handkerchief over his face as if the maid was crying. Then he was smuggled over the sea to France, to be joined later by his devoted wife at the vast and elegant palace at St Germaine-en-laye only 20 miles from Paris and, like Caerlaverock, built in a triangular shape.

There were similar happenings after the Rebellion for the Restoration of the Stuart Kings of 1745. On 26 July in that year the Dumfries Customs collector was informed from Edinburgh that 'James Drummond commonly called Duke of Perth' had made his escape and 'proper directions must be given to our officers to stop him from escaping to parts beyond the seas'. On 12 September it was reported that soldiers of Scots regiments were trying to return to Scotland to join the Jacobite supporters and the Customs men were told to detain them in safe custody until further orders.

A year later the glorious Stuart effort was over and the Customs were informed that the Pretender's son had left the Highlands to escape by sea. All officers were told to be on their guard to watch all creeks and places of embarkation. Bonnie Prince Charlie eventually reached a ship safely—but it was far from the Customs Port of Dumfries.

After the unsuccessful 1745 Rebellion the 'heritable Jurisdiction' which the more important landowners of Scotland had enjoyed over those within their domain was abolished and in 1748 Sheriffs were appointed by the government for the whole country. Compensation was paid for the loss of the privilege and for the loss of income from fines, but as the amounts paid to Lairds on the Solway shore were very small one is left with the suspicion that smugglers had been leniently treated under the traditional Scottish system. For instance, the Maxwell family claimed £6,600 for the loss of their hereditary jurisdiction but were only awarded £523—which possibly reflects how few smugglers had actually been convicted.

On reading the official *Letter Book of the Customs Port of Dumfries* it is apparent that letters were not recorded in either 1715 or 1745. They were possibly removed or, indeed, never entered as the Customs staff, uncertain who would be the winning side, would not wish to commit their allegiance to writing. At both times, however, the Dumfries collectors, John McDowell and John Young respectively, continued in office; so they must have been as loyal as possible to the government of King George.

The Jacobite Rebellion of 1715 found Annan with Lord Johnstone as Provost and John Johnstone of Galabank as Baillie; and since they both supported King George most of the people of Annan followed their lead. Two years previously John Johnstone had sold Galabank, described as 'the vast stone house on the site of Bruce's Castle' (it is now covered by the Town Hall and Council offices) to the magistrates of Annan for public purposes. Thereafter the power of the Johnstone family in the town declined and its place was taken by the merchants of the town, whose loyalty to the throne did not extend to the tax man. Bryce Blair was the first Provost who was not a Johnstone, but he must have been approved by the Earl of Annandale, Chief of the Johnstones.

The provostship may even have been a reward for several loans from the Blairs to John Johnstone (always known as 'Galabank'), who was a direct descendant of Lord Johnstone of Newbie Castle. Today not a single stone remains of this once considerable landmark—possibly because it was poorly rebuilt after the great fire of Christmas 1689 when the entire castle was gutted and the Earl and his wife had to seek shelter at Kinmount.

Three generations of Bryce Blairs have left tantalising glimpses of their varied merchanting and political lives. On 26 February 1689 Bryce Blair was chosen as Commissioner to attend the Convention of Estates held in Edinburgh on 14 March in obedience to the proclamation of William of Orange. He was to receive for his pains £2 16s Scots each day while the convention sat. In 1745 his grandson is recorded as making a forced loan of £100 to Prince Charles Edward Stuart, possibly an insurance in case the Jacobite cause was successful. Then right at the end of the following year, when an outbreak of cattle plague had inflicted great losses on the drovers and the men who financed them, Thomas Bell, a Dumfriesshire drover, wrote from Suffolk to Bryce Blair:

> 'We cannot get money to bear pocket expenses, all hope of selling the cattle is over, our beasts drop in numbers every day, twenty-nine lay dead in one field which should have been worth £5 each. Our conditions are such that several drovers have run from their beasts and left them dying in the lanes and highways with nobody to own them.'

Such were the triumphs and disasters of a family which disappears from the burgh records in 1760 after a century of varied service on the Town Council of Annan. Still many legends lived on of how they masterminded some of the larger smuggling operations—though never personally taking part.

The secret movement of Jacobite families and their servants, as well as princes and priests, by the smuggling boats of the Solway is vividly brought to life in *Redgauntlet*, by Sir Walter Scott. The original Redgauntlets were, of course, the infamous and only too true-to-life family of Grierson of Lagg and Rockhall—already mentioned in this story.

Sir Walter wrote of 'the wretched system which establishes an inequality of duties betwixt the different parts of the same kingdom—a system, be it said in passing, mightily resembling the conduct of a pugilist who should tie up one arm that he might fight the better with the other.'

In *Redgauntlet* we meet the amiable but much feared Father Crackenthorpe, a smuggler from the English side. He is 'as honest a fellow as is of a thousand, a crony of the head borough and constable . . . and the king's exchequer would never bribe a man to inform against him'. Even more important, we meet Alan Fairford, Scott's alter ego, who comes to the Solway shore in search of his young Jacobite friend Darsie Latimer. To gain news of him he must visit Redgauntlet, who is in Cumberland; and the search takes him to Annan (which he describes at length) where he boards the brig *Jumping Jenny* to sail to Silloth.

According to the brig's master, Nanty Ewart, Crackenthorpe 'would drink you a bottle of rum or brandy without starting' but would never wet his lips with 'that nasty Scottish stuff that the canting old scoundrel Turnpenny has brought into fashion'. 'Tam Turnpenny' is the nickname of Tom Trumbull, 'yon hypocritical scoundrel at Annan, who has the best of the profit and takes none of the risk'. Alan Fairford is admitted to Trumbull's premises by a password ending 'Then plague on Aberdeen almanacks'. He descends into an underground maze of cellars where his breathing is affected by the strong smell of spirits and 'other articles of a savour more powerful than agreeable to the lungs'—the Aladdin's cave of spirit casks and contraband wares which filled the hold of the *Jumping Jenny*.

His escort, Job Rutledge, removes an old picture from the wall of a small office in the tunnel, showing a door about seven feet off the ground which in turn leads to a dark and tortuous passage. Another door 'admitted him into a closet, upon the front shelves of which were punch-bowls, glasses, teacups and the like, while on one side was hung a horseman's greatcoat of the coarsest materials, with two great horse-pistols peeping out of the pocket, and on the floor stood a pair of well-spattered jackboots, the usual equipment of the time, at least for long journeys'.

Turnpenny's labyrinth was typical of the kind which was common along the Solway until the middle of the nineteenth century, when duties were equalised. In a note to *Redgauntlet*, Scott stated that 'there was along the frontier an organised gang of coiners, forgers, smugglers, and other malefactors whose operations were conducted on a scale not inferior to what is here described'.

Richard Mendham, originally a carpenter, was one of the ring-leaders of these 'malefactors'. He built a number of houses in Spittal, a suburb of Berwick, and his private mansion was seemingly reached by crossing a series of rooftops and descending through a trapdoor. Beneath his stable was a vault like Trumbull's, entered by another trapdoor. Mendham was tried and executed at Jedburgh: Sir Walter Scott, as Sheriff of Selkirkshire, condemned him.

Annan smugglers

The House of Commons was shocked into action when in 1730 yet another Committee of Inquiry into Smuggling reported that the poor people of the Solway coast could drink tea at a time when only the rich were able to afford such a luxury. Indeed, the Solway people were the first working-class folk to drink tea regularly in Britain, as they could buy smuggled tea—and tobacco too, for that matter—at only half the legitimate market price.

Tea was so expensive that people were tempted not only to smuggle it, but also to counterfeit it. In an attempt to stop this an Act of 1730 laid down that for each 1lb of tea fabricated or manufactured in imitation, mixed, coloured or dyed, there would be a fine of £10. The scale of the problem is revealed by a later government estimate that seven million lbs of tea were smuggled in one year. In a small attempt at control some early leasing deeds of houses along the Solway shore specifically forbade the occupants to engage in smuggling or to be directly or indirectly involved in smuggling or in importing any contraband: 'nor conveying or carrying goods in any way', states a lease of 1763. It may be significant that in the *Old Statistical Account*, where occupations are listed, in some seaside parishes, including Dornock, a considerable number of men are described as 'fishing occasionally'.

Fishing occasionally they might be but the supervisor at the Dumfries Customs house was quite sure that they were up to no good. He sent James Thomson, a Dumfries man, to be tide waiter at Annan as he did not think that the merchants there would 'readily' have quite as much influence over him as others with whom they might be better acquainted.

However, his hopes were short lived. A boat carrying coals from Whitehaven to the Isle of Man arrived at Annan reputedly empty in ballast and Thomson reported that he did not think it necessary to inspect her. The controller immediately posted him to Carsethorn where there was a resident surveyor to supervise him and reported to Edinburgh that Thomson was either lazy and negligent or connived at these practices. As there was no proof of corruption Thomson was not dismissed; but John Bruce a few years later was not so lucky when he claimed payment of two guineas from the Customs board which, he said, he had paid to a pilot to bring the king's cutter from Whithorn to Carsethorn. Their lordships discovered that no pilot had been aboard and in their letter to the collector instructing the dismissal concluded: 'We expect Mr Bruce will trouble us no more'.

In view of the scale of smuggling activity it is not surprising that an indignant Glasgow merchant wrote in 1744:

'We fair traders are much surprised at the neglect of the Officers to let such an illicit trade be carried on by several of this Kingdom and as much encouraged by those of England . . .

'A Dumfries warehouse was broken into by smugglers to regain their property, Collectors of Duty were threatened with their lives by merchants who knew they had the support of smuggling gangs, and knowledge of their whereabouts kept close.

'We shall only mention some of which to our knowledge are a very great detriment to the Government and to us Fair Traders. There are three in company at Annan, the first is John Johnstone the Postmaster, the second is one William Hardie, the other is Tristram Lowther. This John Johnstone is indulged by being the Postmaster, William Hardie is brother in law to Mr Bryce Blair who has a post in the Government and is much indulged by Blair, so that none dare meddle. Lowther is a Cumberland man and well acquainted with the Officers from Carlisle. There is one John Carlyle, one of the greatest smugglers from the Isle of Man, who has a near relation whose name is John Little. The traders in this place often drink his health and tell us how kind he is to them.'

These same men were also referred to in the *Annan Burgh Records* (edited by treasurer Annie Steel in 1933). In 1731 when the Kirk was being repaired the council appointed Bryce Blair to be responsible for the allocation of seats. He was also Provost that year. John Johnstone of Gutterbraes was Provost in 1739 and William Hardie was a town councillor in 1736. Anne Hardie married William Moncrieff, the parish Minister, in 1755. Bryce Blair also appears in the Customs records as a trusted man when he reported that working for the Customs was not an easy life and that the boatmen had constantly to withstand attack, resulting in injuries which needed medical attention. He sent a surgeon's account to the Dumfries collector who then received the following letter from headquarters in Edinburgh:

'DUMFRIES Board to Collector
'24th March 1743
'Having received your letter of the 21st inst. transmitting the account of Mr Robert Feanen, Surgeon, amounting to four pounds seventeen shillings and four pence for his attendance and medicines to James Dickson and James Stewart, Boatmen, who were wounded and bruised in the execution of their duty and it appearing by a letter from Mr Bryce Blair, lykeways enclosed that the said James Stewart is disabled and rendered unfit to row by the loss of some of his fingers and that Archibald Black another of the boatmen is afflicted with a dropsical distemper and thereby incapable to do his duty in the boat. You are to inquire if two of the tydesmen proper for the service will agree to change stations with the said boatmen and to report their answer.'

Ronald Gibbon spent many years researching the Customs and Excise and in a small book published by Whitehaven Museum in 1983, *To the King's Deceit*, tells us that Robert Kneal was sent with his Customs vessel to assist the officers at Carlisle and Annan to move two wherries which had been seized. One of these belonged to Hardie—'the great smuggler'—and had been captured at Carlisle, but smugglers did not surrender their vessels so easily and she was recaptured. Kneal and his crew attempted to seize her again, but the Customs men were attacked by an armed and wicked mob in the night and left for dead. The wherry escaped to the Isle of Man. The ringleaders in the attack were Trusty (presumably a nickname for the aforementioned Tristram) Lowther, John Carlyle, William Curruthers and James Baxter. They escaped over the border and warrants for their arrest were issued in Scotland. Subsequently they were seen at Wigton and on the coast near Allonby where they were said to be carrying on 'a great smuggling trade from the Isle of Man'.

The position of postmaster, held by John Johnstone, had been created in the middle of the seventeenth century when the government messenger route from London to northern Ireland went through Carlisle, via Annan and Dumfries, to Portpatrick. The postmaster was responsible for having horses always available and ready to leave within 15 minutes of the arrival of a messenger from either Carlisle or Dumfries. The carrying of private letters was not firmly organised until 1711 when an Act was passed uniting the postal systems of England and Scotland. The charges were fixed at 2*d* for up to 50 miles.

Dumfries was one of only 12 important post offices in Scotland with a salaried postmaster. He received £12 per annum. Although Annan had a succession of postmasters, there was not a full-time post office there until 1765; and it was another 20 years before the direct mail stagecoach from London ensured delivery to Dumfries within three days. It covered the journey at an average speed of eight miles per hour.

We can appreciate the relative size and importance of Annan in the days of the smugglers largely because of the Reverend Alexander Webster's famous *Census of the Population of Scotland* in 1755. In this census, one of the first in Europe since the fall of the Roman Empire, the population of the Royal Burgh of Annan is reported at 1,498. (The first government census was not taken in Britain until 1801, when Annan's population had grown to 2,500.)

In the Annan district Annan Waterfoot, Newbie, Seafield, Battle-hill and Port Stormont were all noted landing places in their day. At Powfoot, Hill House had been specially built for the smuggling trade, with secret cellars and a good seaward view from its position on top of the hill at the east end of the village: the walls of every room in that house are still lined with wood—and I wonder what secrets have been concealed behind those panels!

In 1760 a riding officer found an unattended horse with a pack of tobacco between Powfoot and Annan. He promptly seized it, later releasing the horse; he was informed that this was wrong and that a repetition of such a generous act would ensure dismissal from the service. Could it be that the officer recognised the horse as one belonging to a friend?

John McLellan, a local lawyer (or writer, as they were then called), left the following account of the burgh of Annan:

'Annan Waterfoot, Newbie, Seafield, Battlehill and Port Stormont, were all noted landing places for contraband goods. There is a vaulted subterranean cellar standing till this day at

Waterfoot, which was used in these times as a depot for smuggled brandy etc . . . At Kenzioles (Back of the Hill, Annan) and other places named, were also depot cellars; and frequently ankers* of liquid were secreted in fields and gardens along the shore. Having been checked by legislation, another system of smuggling sprang up, viz., the carrying of whisky across the Border in skins and tir casks, which has also now ceased, owing to alteration of the Revenue Laws, by a wise equalisation of the duty in Scotland with that of England. Large casks of whisky were brought from Leith by carriers to supply spirit merchants in Annan. Several puncheons would often be disposed of in a night, to gangs who would proceed across the Firth, the difference of duty—4s or 5s a gallon—being the gain for the risk of detection by the Revenue Officers.'

The house at Waterfoot was demolished in 1977, together with

'Annan Waterfoot', by Clarkson Stanfield

many other old buildings; and in 1950 Jim Thomson, who farmed Waterfoot Farm at that time, found an underground room below the floor of a stone-built barn there. It was approximately 30 feet by 15 feet, and 8 feet deep, and was subsequently filled in with rubble and a concrete floor laid. It is also of interest that until the 1940s the narrow

---

*An anker was a cask holding just over eight gallons.

road leading from the Dumfries Low Road down to Powfoot was always referred to as the 'Brandy Loaning'.

When Newbie was mentioned in early documents as a landing place, it is not clear whether the boats unloaded on the open coast near Newbie Castle (now Newbie Mains Farm) or whether they sailed up the River Annan to the sheltered creek where Newbie Mill Burn runs into it. There is now a stone-built footbridge at that point on the Milnefield to Newbie riverside path. Beechgrove, near Annan, also had a tree-shrouded loaning leading down to the sea between Seafield and Battlehill which would have provided cover for smugglers.

Not all trade in Annan was illegal, however. In February 1770 William Kirkpatrick, an Annan merchant, took delivery of a cargo of 1,800 bushels of salt landed by the Duke of Buccleuch for his fisheries at Dornock. Possibly some of this was sold to other salmon stake net owners. A Solway salmon stake net covers several hundred yards of foreshore just above the low water level. At low tide the salmon which have been trapped during high tide are removed. The maze of long, high nets are attached to stakes, 12 to 15 feet long, and remain in position from February to September, storms permitting. To conserve the stocks of fish the traps are open on Saturdays and Sundays, so that the fish may go upriver to spawn.

In 1760 29 worthy men of Annan, led by Captain William Irving of Bonshaw, formed one of the earliest Masonic Lodges in southwest Scotland—Lodge Annan Saint Andrews. In 1767 it was recorded that they went in procession to the place marked out for the brewery, where the Master of the Lodge laid the foundation stone. At this time the traditional Scottish twopenny ale was losing its popularity and being supplanted by the strong ale popular in England and abroad. By the time of the Napoleonic Wars the new breweries were producing large quantities of porter, some of which was shipped to Liverpool and other ports in Lancashire and Cumberland. These products, of course, kept the Excisemen busy measuring (or gauging, as it was called; and the Exciseman was commonly referred to as 'the gauger') to ensure that none escaped duty free. Smuggled spirits, however, was still the favourite local drink!

As others saw us

In your young days ye lookit o'er
Nocht but a dreary barren moor,
Nae house, nae hedge,—wild, rouch, an' poor,
    Wi' scarce a bound,
Whare everybody's beast micht scour
    Ower common ground.

Time's changed, and sae it did betide
The burghers wad the bounds divide,
An' cultivate wi' muckle pride,
    An' biggit beilds;
Noo ye look ower a kintraside
    O' smiling fields.

JOHN PALMER (1800–1870), *To an Old Tree*

John Palmer, who wrote these words in 1850, was Provost of Annan for many years and owner of a successful nursery over 60 acres in extent. His poem tells us of the change in the surrounding country when the town common lands were divided among the Burgesses. Many travellers, too, recorded their journeys and drew attention to the wild, boggy and uncultivated state of Scotland.

One of these travellers, Thomas Pennant, wrote of Annan in his journal in June 1774 as he approached Gretna:

> 'The country now grows very uncultivated and consists of a large common. Reaching Annan a town of four or five hundred inhabitants where vessels of about sixty tons come as high as the bridge. This place has some trade in wine [probably a polite reference to the large smuggling business] and exports between 20,000 and 30,000 Winchester bushels of corn ... Passing over the River Annan on a bridge of five archways defended by a gateway.'

He then rode on to Ruthwell and Dumfries.

The artist Sir Frank Short came to Annan in 1890 to prepare illustrations for a new edition of Sir Walter Scott's *Redgauntlet* and etched the novel's hero, Alan Fairford, entering Annan over a narrow stone bridge, apparently no more than six or seven feet wide with recesses at the side to allow those walking to step back into safety as horsemen passed. Maybe he had seen an old drawing or perhaps he combined his imagination with written details. This bridge had been built in 1701 to replace the town ferry boat which used to cross at the site of the present road bridge. This boat had been let for 100 Markes Scottes (£6 sterling) each year to be operated by John Johnstone of Gutterbraes. Two Englishmen, Parks and Woosly, who contracted to build the bridge, took up smuggling while in Annan but, as they were foreigners, their stock of tobacco on which duty had not been paid was seized and rouped (sold at auction) by the Baillies on 29 August 1701.

To escape paying a toll at every crossing of the bridge, heritors* of Annan willingly paid 1s sterling and tenants 6d sterling for a whole year's use of this, most welcome, bridge.

As late as 1795 the Reverend William McRitchie described Annan in his journal as 'an elegant little cleanly town beautifully situated on the East bank of the River Annan over which there is a good old bridge'. He also referred to the windmill, which ground wheat and other grain, as 'a rare sight in this part of Scotland'. All victuals, he observed, were sold in the town by weight; in Annan one stone was 17 lbs. Wool, however, was sold at the normal weight of 14 lbs to the stone. He further observed the poetic nature of the people, expressed in a publican's sign:

Bread   Beer
Sold   here

The bushel mentioned by Thomas Pennant he defines as 'a measure of capacity' but seldom can there have been a more variable measure. The Imperial bushel contained 8 gallons of liquid or a little over 50 lbs barley and a little over 40 lbs oats. The ancient Winchester bushel was only slightly different, but every town and even parish had its own bushel measure which might again be different. At Penrith it was 20 gallons, in Carlisle 24 gallons; and everywhere it differed according

---

*A freeholder with a liability to contribute to the upkeep of the parish and the parish minister.

to whether it was heaped up or level with the top of the measure. Annan seemed to favour the Winchester bushel. Some merchants even kept two measures; and it was enacted in the city of Carlisle in the reign of Elizabeth I that: 'If any man keep in his house any double measure, that is to say a great one to buy with and a lesser one to sell with, that everyone offending therein shall pay for each offence six shillings and eight pence'. In 1601 Queen Elizabeth issued standard measures and weights—these are now on view in Carlisle Museum. After 1700 a bushel of salt had to contain 56 lbs by weight, no more and no less, said Parliament.

Whether this had the desired effect or not I cannot say; but in 1880 James Shaw, a south-western Scot, penned these lines:

Both when you buy and when you sell,
Look to your weights and measures well;
And when your soul and fingers itch
For pelf, and still you are not rich.
Remember, in the race for gold,
They stumble who rush over-bold.
Keep the plain middle of the way,
And always run with light of day:
Don't break your word, don't tell a lie,
Don't put dust in your neighbour's eye.
And the reward will come with time,
The money bags will clink like rhyme:
The knave and cheat will credit lose,
Whom honest you may then abuse,
Standing high on your own good name,
While up and down there runs your fame, ˎ
And customers beseige your doors
On foot, on horse, in dozens and scores;
Small profits then and many sales,
Like favouring winds will fill your sails . . .

Until around 1945 farmers in this district still ordered their seed grain by bushels, and grain yields were often discussed in terms of the number of bushels per acre. Usually it was oats they grew and a good crop was 50 bushels.

In 1814 Richard Ayton visited the Solway coast on his travels around Britain to prepare a book containing the wonderful illustrations of William Daniell.* Like other visitors he noted the overwhelming connection of the town with the spirit trade, as the following vivid description shows.

'As Annan was the first town that I had the pleasure of seeing in Scotland, I entered it with some curiosity, looking out narrowly for its peculiar marks and distinctions. It is very agreeably situated on an eminence above a fertile valley, watered by the Annan, which, about a mile to the southward, discharges itself into the Solway. The town contains eighteen hundred inhabitants, and consists principally of one broad unpaved street, headed at one end by the gaol with a tower and a spire, and flanked on each side by respectable houses and shops, of various elevations, and jutting out in various degrees of projection, with here and there a hut amongst them, not more wretched, I scarcely think, than some other huts that I have seen, but singular from their being permitted to take their places in the great street. They are built with unhewn stones thrown together as if by accident, and covered with a thatched roof black with rottenness, but giving nourishment to a harvest of rank grass and weeds, and topped by most uncouth chimneys, each formed by four stakes placed about a foot asunder, and wrapped round with bands of straw, or filled up with sods of earth. One is not surprised at seeing such kind of habitations among the wilds of the mountains, where every man builds his house in a Robinson Crusoe-like manner, with any make-shift materials and tools that he can find, but I should really scarcely have expected to find them in a land of bricks and mortar. There are two or three alleys in Annan filled with such huts, excepting which, it has a very creditable appearance, and is not deformed by any of those nuisances which an Englishman is taught to believe are inseparable from the constitution of a Scottish town.

'That whisky is the favourite drink of the people is very evident, not only from the prevalence of red noses, but from a

---

*This journal has been reprinted as *Sailing on Horseback*, edited by Innes MacLeod and published for its great local interest by T. C. Farries and Co Ltd, Dumfries, 1988.

direct notice that it is to be bought at every other house in the place. The vending of it is combined with every other trade, every dealer well knowing that whatever may be his success in other ventures, he is sure of a few customers for this seductive cordial. Opposite to me, as I sat in the inn, I perceived a "draper and dealer in spirits"; a little lower down is a "grocer and dealer in spirits"; and in the town is a still more extraordinary union, a "banker and dealer in spirits". Exclusive of these supplementary dealers, there are plenty of professed publicans, so that a stranger might suspect that this was the great whisky magazine of the nation, till he discovered that in the copiousness of its store, it is only like every other town in Scotland.'

Edward Rickards kept the largest inn in Annan, probably the one which by 1811 had become the Queensberry Arms. In 1798 it was the most heavily taxed building in Annan, with its 30 windows on each of which tax had to be paid. He kept two postchaises and 10 livery horses as well as one sporting dog and seven living-in servants. Altogether it was an important establishment, whose great size is proved by comparison with the local mansion houses—Mount Annan was only taxed on 24 windows and Warmanbie on 13. It is, of course, always possible that the people of this district were as adept at avoiding window tax as they were at avoiding Customs and Excise duties!

The stormy sea

A wet sheet and a flowing sea,
A wind that follows fast
And fills the white and rustling sail
And bends the gallant mast;
And bends the gallant mast, my boys,
While like the eagle free
Away the good ship flies, and leaves
Old England on the lee . . .
The world of waters is our home,
And merry men are we.

ALLAN CUNNINGHAM (1784–1842), *A wet sheet and a flowing sea*

Not only was there a never-ending battle between the revenue men and the smugglers, but there was also the eternal fight against the weather; as the following contemporary description shows:

'A vilent tempest began of Setterday and two or three days the maist tempestuous weather that ever was seen, the sea filling far higher nor ever was seen before in this age, the weather being so tempestuous with extraordinaire graitt waves.'

And the Dumfriesshire poet Allan Cunningham was inspired to pen the lines at the head of this chapter when he spied a smuggling ship raising her sails and speeding away from her secret anchorage.

Then, as now, the Solway claimed the lives of many seafarers—including a fair proportion of smugglers and their accomplices. In the great storm of 1822, over 20 sailing ships sank in the Solway. One of the most serious risks of smuggling was, in fact, shipwreck. A ship-wreck was important news and could not be concealed. So it was vital to send word to the Customs of your honest cargo and seek their help to recover it—rather than let them arrive on the scene and seize the whole cargo and vessel as contraband.

In a case of shipwreck, the tidewatchers recovered any cargo washed up along the shore and protected the goods from pilferers. They also provided certificates of loss to enable insurance claims to be made on the underwriters (who were usually only used for larger boats). An Act of 1719 made the Customs men responsible for pro-tecting all goods from stranded vessels.

In 1742 the town council of Dumfries recognised that there was a great increase in maritime trade (although most of this must have been illegal free traders). They realised that a proper chart of the Solway approaches from Kirkcudbright Bay at Little Ross Island to the Nith was needed—by smugglers, revenue boats and honest traders alike. Thomas Winter produced a most useful and accurate chart and moored a buoy, ordered by the town council from Holland, to mark the channel between the dreaded Barnhourie Sands and the Dumreef Bank in the middle of the Solway.

Improvements continued and in 1747 the Maxwell Earl of Nithsdale gifted six acres of his land to the merchants and shipmasters of Dumfries who had agreed to better the navigation of the Nith by erecting a harbour at Glencaple Burnfoot. This became the principal harbour on the river for the next 200 years. Then road transport took over from the Solway coastal trading ships.

A great deal of smuggling took place at night and the illicit navigators found life a lot easier after 1748 when the magistrates and merchants of Dumfries erected a lighthouse at Southerness. It was not until 1786 that the government-sponsored Commissioners of Northern Lighthouses started their mammoth task of lighting Scotland's seas.

Charts and lights, then as now, could not save all ships from the perils of the sea. Misfortune befell the sloop *Swift* in December 1768 when she was stranded at Newbie, a small distance from the port of Annan. A merchant in Annan, Mr Thomson, requested help from the collector of Customs to save and guard the cargo. His inability to tell the Customs surveyor, David Douglas, the ship's destination aroused certain natural suspicions. For the *Swift* was carrying red and white port, claret and French wines. Wine casks were washed ashore at Carsethorne and at the Blackshaw bank near Caerlaverock: these, and a large quantity found at Newbie, were retrieved by the local tidesmen. The Customs men then sold as much of the wine as would pay the dues of salvage but feared that Thomson would dispute the payment down to the last penny, as after the shipwreck he had already paid the normal import duty as an honest merchant.

Even in midsummer the Solway was a treacherous place. On 23 July another unexpected disaster struck when the king's barge belonging to the Customs Port of Dumfries put to sea with four boatmen to look for sunken casks of brandy. She was lost in entirety and every person aboard perished. On 30 July the collector reported to Edinburgh that the boat had been recovered on the coast of Cumberland and would be sent over to the Carse with the bodies of Mr Craik, Charles Maxwell and John Jardine.

In the following year a very large vessel was sighted approaching the River Annan, whereupon Dumfries mustered all available help. The land surveyor, the land waiter, the riding officer, three tidesmen and six Excise men were convened but no horses could be procured. Since it was the middle of the night the horses might well have been put to a more clandestine use. However, such was the urgency that chaises were hired and arrived at Annan at two o'clock in the morning. Their disappointment must have been considerable when the vessel proved not to be a smuggler after all!

The *House of Commons Journal* reveals the magnitude of the smuggling problem as there are continual references, inquiries, reports and new legislation recorded. In 1744 there was a Royal Proclamation pardoning all smugglers (even murderers) if they joined as common seamen in the fleet. The proclamation seems to have had little effect because the next year the Justices of the Peace were authorised to pursue smugglers into adjoining counties and constables were to raise the 'hue and cry' after any smuggled goods conveyed nearby. Convicted smugglers were condemned to serve five years as common seamen. Thereafter, if they wished to stay in the Navy, they could be promoted.

The Collector writes

If you wake at midnight, and hear a horse's feet,
Don't go drawing back the blind, or looking in the street,
Them that ask no questions isn't told a lie.
Watch the wall, my darling, while the Gentlemen go by!
RUDYARD KIPLING (1865–1936), *A Smuggler's Song*

Two reasons for the lack of control by the Customs and Excise men were the sympathy of the general public for the smugglers and the fact that the officers of the revenue were under staffed. Their requests for military aid often went unheeded. General Wade, for instance, Commander-in-Chief in Scotland from 1722 to 1743, was a wise and humane man who hastened to build roads and bridges which would unite the two kingdoms; but he moved slowly in the enforcement of London laws which would have embittered and divided the two peoples.

In 1725 the government proposed a vast increase in the duty on malt, with the result that there were great riots in Glasgow. Those arrested in the riots were tried for treason, rebellion, and other high crimes and misdemeanours: 'but through the clemency of His Majesty's auspicious and mild Government no capital punishment was inflicted on any of those poor offenders'. After the imposition of this duty vast numbers of illicit stills were set up and continued to flourish for at least the next 100 years.

The problems of controlling the Solway shore are shown in the Customs house records of the day which provide a vivid picture of the excitement of that time.

The collector at Dumfries, Macdouall of Logan, writing to his superiors in Edinburgh on 16 April, relates:

'That two small boats having been hovering on the coast, all the Officers were ordered to be on the look-out, that tracks on the sands of Ruthwell led to a search in that Parish, resulting in the seizure of a secreted cask of brandy, which the Tide-waiters, five in number, were ordered to bring to the Customs House next morning, and that, when they were ready to set out with it, upwards of a hundred women broke the doors and windows of the place where it was kept, and carried off the liquor.

'We humbly lay before your Honours [continues the collector] the necessity of prosecuting such abuses, as well for the security of the Revenue as the protection of the Officers, who are so discouraged that they dare not, without hazard of their lives, go about their duty ... The Ruthwell folks are such friends to the running that they will not for any money give lodgings amongst them to a Revenue Officer.'

An even bolder smuggling affray occurred the following month a few miles further down the coast. A tidewaiter named Young, hearing of some suspicious circumstances, hurried early in the morning to Glenhowan. There he learned from a fisherman that a notorious native smuggler, Morrow of Hidwood, had 'come home' from the Isle of Man. Accompanied by a parish constable, he proceeded to Morrow's house where he found a large pack and two trusses of leaf tobacco. He was just preparing to return with the precious spoil when 'a multitude of women' pounced, vulture-like, upon the captors. The wrathful amazons first dispossessed the constable of the pack which he carried and, while they were running away with it, Young, leaving the trusses to the care of his companion, foolishly set off in pursuit. The consequence may be readily guessed. He might as well have sought to make a troop of wolves give up their prey as persuade these Glenhowan termagents to surrender theirs. The bold rash man of the revenue was soundly beaten by the women and lodged as a captive in the smuggler's stronghold, Hidwood House, till they had secured the whole of the tobacco; after which, sore in mind as well as in body, he was set at liberty.

On reporting himself at headquarters, he was sent back to the scene with a force of 10 men. They searched all the houses, fields and gardens and at length discovered a pack of tobacco in a ditch near Bankend, a village six miles south east of Dumfries; they were hieing homewards with it when lo! another 'monstrous regiment of women', armed with clubs and pitchforks, waylaid the party. Young, thinking to terrify his assailants, shouted out that they would be punished with the utmost rigour for resisting Queen Anne's officers. After a smart conflict the women were put to rout, and the men carried their capture to Dumfries without further disturbance.

In the report of this affair forwarded to Edinburgh much emphasis was laid on the impunity with which the law was defied and its representatives maltreated; and an urgent request was made for the pro-

'Out of sight', by Michael Barton

secution of the offenders and for a troop of dragoons to assist the revenue officers in the execution of their duty. Some of the women were tried at the Circuit Court of Judiciary in Dumfries on a charge of rioting and deforcing the officers; but the witnesses in the case intentionally neutralised their own testimony by professing to entertain malice against the prisoners, and so the latter escaped punishment.

Another report from the Dumfries collector states:

'On the 10th September, 1722, we went to a place called Kirkbride, about seven miles from Dumfries, in pursuance of an information of some brandy lying there. Accordingly we found five small casks of brandy in and about the house of one Andrew Hewitson; and after we had got it upon horseback, and brought it a small way from the house, the said Hewitson raised the whole county upon us, who came with stones, clubs and firearms, and violently deforced us of the said seizure.

'We have reason to believe [adds the Collector] that the representation (made by the Board) is so far true that considerable quantities of foreign spirits, wine, tea and other goods, have been run in our district for many years past, in open boats, from the Isle of Man, that the smugglers run these goods in fleets of boats, ten or twelve at a time, each of which carry twenty-seven or so small casks; that they come in upon the coasts at spring tides in the night, and disperse to different places, that their carriers and assistants are attending upon the shore to receive their cargoes; that they have slings or ropes fitted for their carriage and ride off, and before daylight hide the goods many miles distant from the shore, and no doubt convey the greatest part of them into England.'

Thomas Henderson, who wrote of the history of Annandale, found reports which mentioned large cavalcades of ponies passing not far from Lockerbie and Moffat on their way to the cities of Scotland. It must be remembered that in those days there were many wild tracts of land in Dumfriesshire and Galloway where now there are fertile fields and busy roads. Speed of travel is not the only thing to have changed in 200 years and one wonders if we who live in the bright glare of electric lighting and push-button torches can appreciate the difficulties of all this nocturnal actvity when all that was available was a burning-tar torch and a primitive flint to light it.

Law-abiding citizens preferred not to acknowledge the constant nightly movement of large quantities of goods in many small loads, pretending to turn their faces the other way when the free traders passed so that they could not be called upon by the revenue authorities to identify smugglers; and to restrain the curiosity of their children they invented tales of ghosts and goblins to explain the sounds of man and beast which wakened children in the night.

The Salt Duties

In the fourteenth century Robert the Bruce rewarded the people of Ruthwell—a small village between Dumfries and Annan—for aiding him by giving them the right to make salt on their part of the Solway shore. At a time when practically all salt was produced by the evaporation of sea water, Ruthwell's salt-making was a major industry. When a duty on salt was introduced in Scotland by King James I of Scotland in 1428, he respected the rights of the people of Ruthwell by exempting their salt from the tax. However, much later Oliver Cromwell—who had no respect for royal decrees—in 1656 levied a duty on them; this was removed by Charles II but reinstated by Queen Anne in 1708, although in deference to the old tradition it was only at one-third of the rate levied in England.

The statutes relating to salt contain a wealth of information with many interesting glimpses of associated matters which were tacked on to these Acts of Parliament merely as a convenience, such as the clauses added in 1707 'to enable Her Majesty to dispose of the effects of William Kidd, a notorious pirate, for the use of Greenwich Hospital'. Or that added in 1730 to grant repayment of duty to an executor for a large loss of salt caused by the overflowing of a river. Possibly some merchants of Dumfries were also compensated when the Nith flowed into their warehouses.

The English salt duty had been a small charge which neither upset those who paid nor those who collected it; until the fateful year of 1694, when substantial increases of duty on salt, beer, ale and other liquors were granted to the then impecunious King William III and Queen Mary II.

The Act said:

'We your majesties most Loyal and Dutiful subjects, the Commons in Parliament assembled being sensible of the great and necessary expense in which your majesties are engaged in carrying on the present war against the French King and being desirous to supply the same in such manner as may be least grievous to your majesties' subjects. Be it enacted that throughout the Kingdom of England the Dominion of Wales and the town of Berwick upon Tweed the rates and duties for Salt will be as follows:-

'All salt imported into these ports 3*d* per gallon over and above the present duty.

'All Rock Salt or Pit Salt produced in the realm 1*d* per gallon.'

The Commissioners of Excise were made responsible for the collection from owners of rock salt or makers of pit salt, who were not allowed to permit salt to be moved without an Excise ticket. Thus it became worthwhile to smuggle salt from Scotland to England. This was even more attractive three years later when the duties were increased and, as with all smuggled goods, as the duties increased so also were the measures to prevent increased evasion.

The old measurement of eight gallons to a bushel was found to be 'various, unequal and inconvenient' to all except those who were making a profit out of the uncertainty; so it was enacted that all quantities of salt except rock salt should be calculated at 56 lbs to the bushel—rock salt was 75 lbs to the bushel, but in 1702 this was reduced to 65 lbs per bushel.

In 1695 a penalty of £10 was ordained for anyone refusing to give evidence before a Justice on any offence against the Excise, and any duty so collected was to be divided between the king and the informer. Later that year duties upon salt, glassware, stone and earthenware and tobacco pipes were reviewed. After 25 March 1698 no person was allowed to sell salt except by weight. On conviction of evasion £5 had to be forfeited to the informer but buyers of salt other than by weight also had to forfeit 10*s* for every bushel not weighed.

In 1699 the duty was further increased on imported salt to 10*d* per gallon, and on home-produced salt to 5*d* per gallon. This encouraged more smuggling and to counter this it was enacted that officers might seize salt being conveyed without warrant by day or night and by land or sea. If not claimed within 10 days it was utterly forfeit; or, if claimed and the claimant was unable to prove that the goods had been entered at the Excise office, forfeited at double its value. This caused violent reaction; and the penalty for beating or obstructing an Excise officer was increased to £20 for each offence.

After Queen Anne's accession in 1702 it became the responsibility of every maker or refiner of salt to make an entry at the salt office of the number and situation of every salt pit, work, pan, storehouse or warehouse made use of by him, on pain of forfeiting the sum of £40: and persons living near the salt work or sea coast who refused to claim ownership of salt found in their custody or to identify the owner were to pay double the value, plus 10s per bushel, unless they could prove from whom they had bought it. It was found that these people were usually so poor that they could pay neither the duty nor the fine; so it was enacted that where duty had not been paid the salt would be forfeit, and must be redeemed by payment of duty within 10 days—otherwise the offender's goods would be sold and, if they were not of sufficient value, the offender would be imprisoned. Those who had no money to pay the fines were to be sent to the house of correction to be whipped and kept to hard labour for up to a month.

Also in 1702 new commissioners were appointed whose responsibility was specifically the management of the salt duties; and no dealer in salt was allowed to act as a Justice of the Peace in matters relating to the Salt Acts.

Masters of ships carrying salt along the coast were carefully watched in case they added to their cargo between ports some salt on which duty had not been paid. However, any ship carrying salt which was seized or sunk as an act of war enabled the shipper to buy the same quantity free of duty. An oath had to be sworn that it had been taken on board at a home port in England, Wales or Berwick (not from Scotland, Ireland or a passing ship). Pilchards packed in barrels for sale had to have the name of the owner and the number of pilchards in each cask burned on the cask—many sealed casks had been found to conceal smuggled goods. The use of brine or rock salt for curing flesh or fish was prohibited until the salt had been refined and duty paid on it. Many frauds were practised by curing fish at sea with non duty-paid salt. Scottish salt conveyed to England was liable for the full foreign duty and had to be entered either at Carlisle or at Berwick-upon-Tweed, otherwise it was forfeit at double its value plus 20s per bushel.

Any vessel laden with salt found hovering on the coast and not proceeding on her voyage could be boarded by a salt officer and allowed a maximum of 20 days' stay in port. After that the salt had to be entered and duty paid. It was so easy for small boats to hide among the fishing boats that it was decided that the minimum size of vessel allowed to import salt should be 20 tons burthen.

In 1704 the Isle of Man is first mentioned in Acts to control the smuggling of salt; also for the first time, not only the salt but the ship and tackle putting unduptied salt on shore became liable to forfeiture. Not content with these harsh measures, Parliament decreed that people helping to land salt or to carry it away could be imprisoned for up to six months.

After 5 June 1704 no salt was permitted to be brought out of Scotland into England by land, on pain of forfeiture plus a fine of 20s per bushel, but English salt exported to Scotland, the Isle of Man, Jersey or Guernsey, was entitled to a drawback—ie a repayment of some duty to bring it down to the lower level existing in Scotland before the Union of the Parliaments. Encouragement was also given to fishermen with the courage to sail across the Atlantic to Newfoundland by the exemption of their catch from salt duty.

The Act of Union between Scotland and England gave certain undoubted advantages to Scottish trade. It provided for a subsidy of 10s 5d for every barrel of white herrings exported from Scotland; and for seven years Scottish-made salt was to be exempt from part of the English duty. This advantage, however, had to be restricted in the face of loud complaints from English merchants.

This in turn brought complaints from the Scots. As farmers in this part of Scotland were dependent on the English market they were indignant that among the measures taken was one saying that salt used for curing Scottish meat intended for export to England or beyond the seas had to pay the full English duty, in order to establish an equality of trade. Most of the exports from the Dumfries Customs area went by ship to Liverpool, and as a result of the salt law more cattle and sheep were sent alive, while pigs were killed and cured locally and exported salted.

It was obvious by 1710 that one of the results of the Act of Union was a great increase in the smuggling of salt; and varied measures were introduced by Parliament in an attempt to control it. These included a uniform allowance for waste of salt for seaborne voyages of over 20 miles, which was fixed at three bushels for every 40 carried; the waste salt had to be thrown overboard in the presence of the salt officer. Seized goods had often been claimed by a nominee who had no assets to lose, so in future a security of £30 was demanded of any claimant. However, to be fair to both sides any defendant found not guilty was to be awarded double costs; this was to discourage vindictive or groundless complaints.

From 1714 the full duty was paid on Scottish salt, less the 2s 4d per bushel imposed by the English Parliament in 1659, a lower rate which continued at least until 1734 when it was again confirmed—probably at 1d per gallon, compared to the 5d which was due in England. Notwithstanding the many complaints, the Scottish salt industry was more prosperous after the Union as it flooded the north of England market both with its lower-taxed salt and with some that had paid no tax at all.

By 1719, when George I was on the throne, the government realised that the fishing industry provided many loopholes for the evasion of duty and a further succession of regulations was introduced. They started with the fishery proprietor, who had to pay 20s for every bushel of salt taken out of his cellars and not accounted for. Then, when he had caught the fish, they had to be packed in barrels of a size uniform throughout Britain, with the owner's name burned on the barrel. Barrels for herring contained 32 gallons and those for salmon 42 gallons, but a few years later half-barrels were allowed in order to pack ships' holds better. However, this was not effective so exported fish had to have part of their tails cut off and, if relanded in Britain, were forfeit. At the same time the herring salt duty was replaced by a duty of 1s 8d per 1,000 fish. White herrings could still be computed at 3s 4d per barrel, but all the Acts reiterated the insistence that Scottish ships must obey the Salt Laws—a sure sign that they had not been doing so!

In the same year a new, and more onerous, office was placed on the Customs service, to help and protect all vessels wrecked or stranded on the shores of Britain; reasonable salvage charges were paid first, then the duty and the balance were held for the benefit of the owner. It was then discovered that by reason of the very high duties on some foreign goods it was more profitable to have them condemned for sale. This often took place at a ridiculously low price to the person who had in fact imported them and who should have paid the high duty; worse still was the fact that half the sale price went to the informer who had discovered the whereabouts of the cargo. Often the collusive seizure was made by a Customs officer who had, in the words of the Act, 'received a moderate gratification'. In future any officer making a collusive seizure was to be fined £500 and lose his job.

Three years later, in 1722, three more regulations were made. The first made prosecution mandatory for any ship's master getting duty-free goods from other ships at sea. The next ordered that persons running brandy etc, who were caught, could no longer escape the law by removing to another county and using an assumed name but were now to be pursued. Lastly, as the cost of the Customs service was growing fast, to try to reduce the costs of keeping seizures it was enacted that vessels under 15 tons, also horses, cattle and carriages used in conveying this illegal trade could be condemned by the judgement of any two Justices of the Peace—it was no longer necessary to wait for the Quarter Sessions.

By 1730 the government of Walpole appeared to be learning from bitter experience that the only lasting cure for smuggling was to reduce duties. Those on salt produced in Britain were abolished after 25 December, while duties on imported salt were reduced by seven-tenths—altogether a wonderful Christmas gift for everyone except the smugglers! This Act had an additional and important effect on the Customs Port of Dumfries as all salt duties were henceforward to be collected by the Customs service, rather than by the Excise.

Sanity, however, was short lived. A need for money persuaded Parliament to revive all the salt duties with their host of regulations on 25 March 1732. As a gesture to Scotland, salted white herrings could be brought to England on payment of 2s 4d per barrel of 32 gallons at the port of landing—a reduction of 1s on the previous charge.

In 1736 the 'Desperation Act', as it was described by the opposition, laid down that foreign goods taken in or put out of any vessel within four leagues of the coast (unless in dire necessity) were to be forfeited and the masters of both vessels were to forfeit treble the value of the goods; also the boats, if under 100 tons, would be forfeit. When the case came to trial the judge was directed to proceed to the merits of the case without inquiring into the fact or the form of the seizure. This would indicate that the lack of convictions was upsetting the government—as it continued to do for the next 100 years.

The commissioners of Customs collected the salt duties until 1798, when responsibility was returned to the board of Excise; this lasted until 1825, when this tax on one of the necessities of life was abolished—which must have been a great relief to the poor people, who had suffered most.

Lingtowmen and others

Gin by pailfuls, wine in rivers,
Dash the window-glass to shivers!
For three wild lads were we, brave boys,
And three wild lads were we;
Thou on the land, and I on the sand,
And Jack on the gallows-tree!
SIR WALTER SCOTT (1771–1832), *Guy Mannering*

Many more people on land than at sea were involved in the smuggling trade. There were those who financed cargoes, those who watched for the boats' arrival, signallers from the shore and those who, men, women and children, unloaded the goods, then concealed and transported them. Each hogshead was split into 20 sacks for ease of handling and hiding and these were carried by the Lingtowmen, so called because of the special rope slings they used to fasten the bales or kegs across the horses' backs, two horses per man. There were, too, depot keepers on the hill routes to the cities, who had to contend with the less sympathetic inland communities. On one of the lonely roads from the Solway to Sanquhar a farmhouse built by a retired merchant on the Duke of Buccleuch's estate has a large stone cellar beneath the study floor, where valuable goods could be concealed.

The town council of Sanquhar recorded in 1730 that the smuggling of brandy and spirits was being practised in the burgh to some extent, and that the Provost, baillies, council and deacons of trades were taking into consideration 'the pernicious effects of the clandestine importation and open consumption of brandy within this Burgh and neighbourhood thereof. And appearing evidently to them that considerable sums of money are yearly expended for purchasing this unnecessary commodity. And being resolved for the good of this Burgh to take an effectual course for the time to come, do therefore statute and ordain that no person or persons within this Burgh shall import, resett, sell or retail brandy or foreign spirits contrary to law, certifying hereby the contraveener or contraveeners that they shall not only be and hereby liable to a fine of five pounds sterling for every such offence, but also declared incapable of bearing any public office in the Burgh in time coming.'

It was reported that on the Solway shore 'there was neither legitimate trade nor industry, and brandy ran like well-water', but smuggling did not only affect the coast of Dumfriesshire and Galloway; it permeated the whole area. Young men gave up steady work as fishermen, farmers or craftsmen to earn easier money, and for excitement tinged with heroics. On the eastern side of the county the overland routes to England were busy. In 1752 the Scottish Board of Customs placed six riding officers on the borders in an attempt to reduce the flow of spirits, tobacco, tea and silks into England. This had little effect. In 1782 it is recorded that Customs officers, supported by Dragoons from Annan, seized nearly 10,000 lbs of tobacco in dealers' stores at Langholm and Gretna. The collector at that time claimed that a company called McDowal and Co had established a warehouse at Sarkfoot to handle illicit cargoes. There must, however, have been several merchants there, for in September 1769 the *Speedwell*, under the command of Captain Bell, was reported to be unloading wines from Guernsey at Sarkfoot for Mr Malcolm, a merchant there.

Torduff Point, between Dornock and Gretna, was frequently mentioned in reports by the collectors on both sides of the Solway because of its lawless enterprising inhabitants who in 1747 murdered William Pasley, an English Customs officer, near Rigg. But no matter how lawless some of the land smugglers might be, the men of the Solway had a good heart for sailors and never at any time did they try to wreck ships—as those evil jackals did around much of England and Wales when they tried to lure innocent ships on to the rocks where they could despoil them. The Solway men, at least, were described as 'honest rogues'!

At Balcary Bay, the opposite end of the coast controlled by the Customs Port of Dumfries, a large and ostentatious house, stores and underground cellars were built by an important company of smugglers, Messrs Clark, Crain and Quirk. This was an enterprising firm managed by the lean and eager Quirk who, hearsay records, was better known as the head of a County family. Such was the continuing ability of a later generation in the firm that when smuggling declined they sold it to the projectors of the Ayrshire and Galloway Railway as being suitable for a large port with a terminus of the railway! The large cellars, with walls five feet thick and doors opening towards the sea, can still be seen at Balcary Bay Hotel—clear proof that the smugglers felt no need to conceal their trade except at the moment of unloading in case the vessel itself should be seized.

Although the bay, with Heston Isle sheltering it, is beyond the River Urr, the tidewatcher at Auchencairn, beside the bay, was attached to Dumfries at various times. Near Balcary Point is a natural rock seat, known as Adam's Chair from a tradition that a smuggler of that name used to sit there in the darkness of the night with a lantern to guide the smuggling boats safely to the shore, either in Balcary Bay or a little further west in the great caves of Barlocco, which are the largest on this coast. (The Black Cave is 256 ft long and the White Cave 252 ft.) So many sailing vessels perished on the Barnhourie sands that Balcary Bay was later laid open and declared a free port of refuge by an Act of Parliament.

Often the Lords Commissioner in Edinburgh inquired why seized ships had not been sailed to Dumfries port and sold or broken up. In 1805 the collector had to explain that the *Elly Anne* had been so badly damaged that he had sent two men to Annan Waterfoot to supervise her being broken up. It took from 11 am to 10 pm, but only cost £2 0s 4d which, he trusted, was the most economical course. Another boat, the sloop *Nancy*, had been damaged in a storm and would have cost more to repair than she was worth, so she was broken up at Glencaple. The cost of a gig to convey the deputy collector and his refreshment to the scene was 10s 6d. The hulls of seized vessels had still to be sawn and burned and a certificate of burning sent immediately to Edinburgh.

Fifty years on

Half a century of work by the preventive services had had little impact on smuggling and nothing describes the state of Kirkcudbrightshire (the neighbouring county to Dumfriesshire) in 1760 better than the report of the Dumfries collector to Edinburgh which said: 'Now they ride openly through the country with their goods in troops of 20, 30, 40 and sometimes 50 horses. Suffering no Customs officers to come near to try a discovery of who they are, far less to seize their goods.'

He goes on to ask for a company of Highlanders to be stationed in the town: 'A military force is absolutely necessary for suppressing the audacious practice of smuggling'.

The use of troops, however, caused many disputes over rewards and 20 years were to pass before King George III issued a decree, in 1780: 'His Majesty Authorises, Directs and Commands that twelve and a half per cent of all goods seized by help of the army shall be paid to the soldiers and officers concerned.'

The same story of impotence was described by Joseph Train, who became supervisor of Excise at Annan and was a regular correspondent of Sir Walter Scott, telling him about the Solway people, among whom was the notorious smuggler Captain Yawkins. Sir Walter's Waverley novels, especially *Guy Mannering* and *Redgauntlet*, give a lucid insight into the practice of smuggling, through fictionalisation of real-life characters. The elusive Dirk Hatteraick of *Guy Mannering*, ace pirate and minor folk hero, was based on the bold Captain Yawkins.

Yawkins was a Dutchman who lived in the Isle of Man and sailed his luggers, the *Black Prince* and the *Hawk*, up and down the Solway with impunity for many years. He preferred not to come as far up as Annan but stayed further west where there was more sailing room to elude the revenue cutters. Yawkins, 'half Manks, half Dutchman, half devil', used to land his contraband wares along the rugged coast of Galloway. Train reported of one of his more daring exploits, the landing of illicit cargo at Manxman's Lake near Kirkcudbright in defiance of two revenue cutters which were bearing down on him:

'The dauntless freebooter instantly weighed anchor and bore down right between the cutters, so close that he tossed his hat on the deck of one and his wig on that of the other, hoisted a cask to his maintop to show his occupation, and bore way under an extraordinary pressure of canvas without receiving injury'.

Train also tells us that in the halcyon days of free trade the price for carrying a box of tea or a bale of tobacco from the Solway coast to Edinburgh was around 15s, and a man with two horses carried four such packages. Such long, frequent and dangerous journeys could only be made because most of the people of Scotland, from the land-owners down, were in sympathy with the free traders. However, it was rare for any but the ordinary people to be searched or arrested. Even so, those who were arrested were not too troubled as they knew that several county Justices and burgh magistrates were deeply involved in the trade, and that a much larger number were at least sympathetic to the smugglers and their carriers.

Samuel R. Crockett was born in Galloway. After a short spell as a minister he became a most popular author; in 1895 he wrote *The Raiders*, in which one of his characters, Lady Grizel Maxwell, expresses the position by saying: 'A keg ower the back o' the dyke is yae thing but cellars full o' brandy is anither'. The keg was very acceptable!

Crockett also tells how Captain Yawkins flouted the Navy and Customs cutters once too often so they gathered a small flotilla from which he could not escape. He was captured and taken to the High Court in Edinburgh and condemned to be hanged on the gibbet at Leith Sands. The more important smugglers were taken to Edin-burgh for trial as it was rare for a court in Dumfriesshire or Galloway to convict unless the offence took place on a Sunday—the Kirk Ses-sions took a serious view of Sabbath-breaking and a public rebuke before the congregation left the magistrate with little option but to convict.

Yawkins' many legendary exploits were not due to luck or the devil but more likely through his study of the wind. He only made land-ings when the breeze was blowing from the land and at the approach of a revenue boat beating in against the wind he commanded the shore party to push as his crew hoisted sail so that he could be away with the wind before the king's ship could alter course. However, one night in 1787 when Yawkins was ashore at Dundrennan Burnfoot his

65

ship, the *Hawk*, was taken with her cargo of 89 boxes of tea, 400 casks of spirits, silks and tobacco—a very valuable cargo, as was to be expected of Yawkins. Whether he was in fact captured as Crockett relates I do not know; but it is recorded that the *Hawk* was not considered sufficiently seaworthy to be converted to a revenue ship.

Among the tricks tried by the less flamboyant smugglers to elude the revenue men was to roll spun tobacco round the body, which worked well for thinner people. Stouter smugglers, however, were soon spotted and carried off to the Customs house. Six lbs weight of tobacco was the legal dividing line between petty smuggling, punished by a fine, and commercial smuggling, which was treated with greater severity. Fishermen who concealed kegs under water beside their nets and brought them ashore with the fish were more successful, not only in evading the Customs, but also in evading punishment; because if discovered they could claim with a great show of innocence that their nets had accidentally brought the kegs up. As did all other smugglers, they suffered from the forfeiture of the goods, but this was looked on more as an inconvenience than a punishment—and some might receive a reward for discovering the contraband. The seizure and later sale of a horse would also be both an inconvenience and a punishment until it could be bought back—probably at a knock-down price as no one else would bid for it.

One of the accepted ways of avoiding paying full duty was for ships' masters and, of course, the merchants involved, to understate the quantities of cargo for it was not easy to check how much was off-loaded on to each cart, particularly with such things as timber and sugar. Another vexatious problem for the Customs men was the number of claims by captains that part of their cargo had been damaged in a storm, when the collector, accompanied by two independent merchants, had to assess what quantity deserved a reduction of duty. In one particular instance, from a total of 213 half pipes of Spanish wine (53 tuns and 58 gallons) the following was agreed: 71 were sound; 98 were one-third part damaged; 44 were one-quarter part damaged. Obviously this resulted in a substantial reduction of the potential duty payable.

A tun barrel held 252 gallons of wine, equal to two pipes or four hogsheads. In the case of that other much-smuggled commodity, tobacco, the hogsheads in which it was brought from Virginia to the

'High and dry', by Michael Barton

Isle of Man could contain as much as half a ton. In Man they were broken down into smaller packs before being landed on the mainland.

The *Edinburgh Evening Courant*, which appeared on three evenings a week, carried extracts of news from the London papers—which must have been at least four days late as it took the London to Edinburgh fly that length of time to make the journey in good weather—and also from letters sent by people from all parts of Scotland and the rest of Europe, often reported smuggling exploits:

'13 April 1772:
'One of this morning's papers says that the two notorious Kennedies who were transported for smuggling in the Solway bred a mutiny in the transport ship which was carrying them to Maryland and butchered the Captain with remarkable barbarity.'

23 April 1774:
'Extract from a letter from Stranraer, dated April 20th:
'Yesterday the Cumbrey Cutter, *Captain Crawford*, arrived from a cruise and brought up a smuggling wherry fully loaded with a valuable cargo of spirits and tea from North Faro.'

The paper also printed a wide variety of advertisements, including this interesting one from 13 July 1774, and placed by the Customs house:

'By order of the Honourable the Comissioners of His Majesty's Customs To be exposed For Sale at the Customs Houses of the ports and upon respective days undermentioned at the hour of twelve each day:

'For Home Consumption, sundry parcels of spirits, tea, coffee-berries, red French wine, red and white Portugal wine, white Spanish wine, vinegar, china ware, soap, groceries and ships furniture.

'For Exportation, silks, silk handkerchiefs, cambricks and playing cards condemned in His Majesty's Court of Exchequer.

'Dunbar   19 July 1774
Prestonpans   20 July 1774
Leith   21 July 1774
Kirkcaldy   26 July 1774
Perth   27 July 1774
Montrose   28 July 1774
Aberdeen   29 July 1774
Thurso   30 July 1774
Port Glasgow   3 August 1774
Ayr   4 August 1774
Stranraer   5 August 1774
Wigtown   6 August 1774.'

The bumper years

After the middle of the eighteenth century the smuggling trade continued to thrive and grow for 30 years. Seizures became larger. In 1776 a smuggling cutter was caught north of the Isle of Man with a cargo of spirits and tea worth no less than £2,000, and some of the cargoes that got through were even larger.

The Dumfries Customs men realised that if they were to win they must try to control the landowners and the lawyers, most of whom engaged enthusiastically in the trade. Merchant smugglers were seldom praised publicly but in the *Literary History of Galloway* there is great praise for a Mr McHarg 'who dealt chiefly in contraband tea'. Others were not so regarded! Sheriff substitute John Welsh landed three chalders of coal at Caerlaverock without the presence of an officer, but a tidesman spotted it and Welsh had to ride quickly to Dumfries to make an entry at the Customs house and pay the coal duty. Around the same time Mr Dickson, Laird of Locharwoods, was caught bringing in coal by sea and he also had to hasten to the Customs house to make his peace. Even so, the Customs surveyor seized both their boats, the *Welcome* and the *Dolly*, and refused to release them until he had permission from Edinburgh. Edinburgh agreed to release the boats but commended both the surveyor and the tidesman for their devotion to duty; and warned Welsh and Dickson that their position in society would not save them in future.

In desperation the sheriff decided to take strong action to try to stem the flow of smuggled goods. The *Weekly Magazine*, the first Dumfries local paper, reports the trial of John Forest from The Back of the Hill, Annan. He was found guilty of having in his possession a quantity of spirits for which he could not account. The sheriff sentenced him to jail for three months, until 28 May, when he was to be publicly whipped through the streets of Dumfries in the following manner:

> 'to be tied to a cart to receive thirty lashes at the foot of the Bridge Vennel, thirty at the head of it, thirty opposite the prison, thirty at the Fish Cross and thirty at the Kirkgate Port and thereafter remanded to prison until the 28th August upon which day to undergo the same punishment again, then to be banished from the County for life'.

Similar treatment for twentieth-century drug smugglers could prove to be salutary!

There was also a new plan under consideration by the commissioners of the Customs and Excise, to offer a handsome reward for the discovery of all persons involved in smuggling goods and also those having smuggled goods concealed in their houses.

In the autumn of 1778 a well mounted gentleman and his servant rode into Dumfries and put up at the County Hotel—where Bonnie Prince Charlie once stayed. For a few days they treated all with generosity, visiting several hostelries, and rumour soon spread that there were some very important smugglers in town. Rumour could not have been more mistaken. On the Monday the gentleman went to the long room of the Customs house to discuss business with Robert Maxwell, the collector, where he caused great consternation by finally introducing himself as Mr Bird, the Inspector General of Customs. He had unearthed no criminal practices but a careless slackness that astounded and enraged him. He instantly dismissed two tidesmen and sent a full report to Edinburgh where the Lords Commissioner acted immediately: for the first and last time in the turbulent history of the Dumfries Port the collector was dismissed.

With Robert Maxwell, the collector, went: George Gordon, the land surveyor; Thomas Corbett, the riding officer; and John Graham and Alex Brown, tidesmen. Mr Ewart, the comptroller, escaped with a reprimand owing to his advanced age and infirmity.

A Mr Anderson was appointed interim collector 'to hold the keys of the King's Chest and to reform the bad practices which had prevailed at the Port of Dumfries'. He was succeeded by Willwood Maxwell who, however, did not satisfy the Inspector General; in December 1780 he was replaced by David Staig, whose first decade in office saw a great reduction in smuggling—increased taxes then caused an increase in smuggling. Staig's was a ceaseless battle until he retired after a record-breaking 33 years as collector of Customs in the port of Dumfries.

David Staig was one of the most remarkable men in the story of Dumfries. William McDowall in his *History of Dumfries* wrote:

'At Michaelmass 1783 a gentleman was elevated to the Provostship, who for more than a generation afterwards took a leading part in public affairs—Mr David Staig. If during that time anybody deserved to be termed King of Dumfries it was he.'

Mr Staig's word was law. Among his many duties he represented the Bank of Scotland in the burgh for almost 40 years. On becoming Provost for the first time he advocated an Act of Parliament to improve the town and, along with a Mr Aitken, he went to London and obtained a Police Act to provide for the paving, cleansing, lighting and policing of the burgh, which at that time had a population of about 5,500. His work was so highly appreciated that he was elected Provost on no fewer than 10 different occasions; he was Provost for 18 years between 1783 and 1817.

One of his most difficult times was during the crop failures of 1795 when he took a leading part in purchasing 26,000 stones of meal to help feed the hungry townspeople. During the bread riots of that winter it was said that Provost Staig 'was the pilot who weathered the storm'. The *Dumfries Monthly Magazine* of October 1826 recorded his death at the age of 84, the only surviving Deputy Lieutenant of the county originally appointed. It is an interesting coincidence that the same page records the death at Ryedale Cottage, Troqueer, Dumfries, of John Lewars, late supervisor of Excise, aged 57 years.

At the close of the eighteenth century the Annan tidewatcher was George Brown, who lived at Summergate where he had a clear view of the Solway and the mouth of the River Annan. Summergate remained a row of five cottages until 1930 when my father bought them and reduced them to four so that bathrooms could be installed. One house was given an upstairs room whose dormer window would have been ideal for George Brown with his telescope!

His first recorded exploit was early in 1797 when he heard that a Manx boat was smuggling salt at Cummertrees Pow. Along with Mr Caddenhead, the Excise officer, he employed William Elliott and Francis Carruthers, both seamen in Annan, to accompany him to assist in seizing the boat. All went well and they were able to row out and board before the smugglers realised their danger. Elliott and Carruthers then refused to help—and stayed on board, drinking with the Manxmen! Brown and Caddenhead were forced back into their small boat and sent ashore deprived of their easy seizure. Not surprisingly Brown expressed considerable indignation when in 1802 Elliott was appointed a full-time tidesman.

In 1803 Brown was ordered to take extreme action against a number of Annan fishing boats which were not named on their stern as required by a new Act. He gave them 14 days to comply on pain of seizure of the boats, together with oars, masts and sails; needless to say, such dire threats brought quick results.

Tidesmen, tidewaiters or tidewatchers as they were also called, continued to be used until about 1870, by which time practically all ships docked at approved quays and vessels no longer beached at any convenient cove as they had done on the Solway coast in the eighteenth century when there were few solid quays at which to moor, and most of the boats were rather flat keeled. They used to take the bottom as near to the shipper's house or store as possible and unload at low tide. It was an important part of a skipper's knowledge to know how far up he could beach his boat with certainty of getting off the next day and not being stranded until the next big tide.

There was no sadder sight than a crew and all the available helpers pushing and pulling vainly at a boat which was aground. It is easy enough today for a yachtsman to miss the tide, even with the help of tide tables; but with a difference of almost an hour for high water on the short coastline of the Dumfries port there was a real risk of being caught on a neap tide. This could bring considerable financial loss to a trading ship, which might have to wait several days for a high tide to float her back to business—and could be total disaster for a smuggler.

The ebb and flow of the smuggling tide

Among the many government schemes to stop smuggling was an Act of 1779, introduced by William Pitt the Younger, which empowered the seizure of any rowing boat with more than six oars if found, either on land or water, within two leagues of the coast of Great Britain. This was only one of many articles of an increasingly chaotic legislation embracing somewhere like 1,000 Acts of Parliament, most of which had little effect.

The basic problem was the high level of duty and there was little progress in eliminating smuggling until the government of William Pitt the Younger passed sensible Acts of Parliament which, by reducing the duties on certain key goods, eradicated the most profitable elements of the smuggling trade. Pitt may well have been encouraged in this by Adam Smith, author of *The Wealth of Nations*, who was appointed a commissioner of the Scottish Customs in 1778. In his famous book Smith blamed parliament rather than the smugglers for the free trade. He wrote: 'He would have been in every respect an excellent citizen had not the laws of his country made that a crime which nature never meant to be so . . .'

Pitt instigated this legislation by reporting to parliament that:

'the several duties on tea amount together to such a considerable amount in proportion to the value of the commodity that they encourage fraudulent importation, illicit practices and dangerous consequences to the public, the prevention of which is of the utmost importance'.

Duty was reduced to 12 per cent of the price at which tea was sold by the East India Company (it ranged in price from 1s 6d to 4s 6d per pound wholesale). Licences were introduced for the makers of dutiable goods such as brewers, maltsters, brandy dealers, calico printers, and candlemakers. The strongest blow against the smugglers, however, was that duties on some wines and spirits for home consumption were discontinued for two years. Worse was to come: should vessels carrying spirits or wine come within four leagues of the shore without due cause they would be forfeit (both ship and cargo); and anyone shooting at a naval, Customs or Excise officer should suffer death as a felon. Some were forced by these laws to give up smuggling—but many continued, albeit on a smaller scale.

The immediate effect of Pitt's legislation was recorded for posterity (a rare occurence in the secret world of smuggling) when the first *Statistical Account of Scotland* was prepared. This was the responsibility of every parish minister and several reported, clearly with mixed feelings, that the decay of smuggling occasioned by the recent Acts had increased the number of paupers who had to be supported by the parish. Indeed, some ministers defended their parishioners' illegal occupation by saying that notwithstanding the many temptations from the abundance and variety of foreign spirits illegally imported on their coast they had always provided well for their families.

One Annandale minister is reputed to have told a visitor that his wife received her tea by having it passed from hand to hand through the hedge because she did not want her neighbours to know of her wasteful indulgence in such an expensive beverage; however, I feel that her real reason was that she agreed with Adam Smith's views and was buying cheap, smuggled tea!

George Maxwell of Munches decided to take positive steps to deal with the independent spirit of the people in his parish of Urr. He built the new town of Dalbeattie in 1780, where he offered every feuer (property-holder) a supply of peats close at hand so that they did not need to smuggle coal across the Solway. A paper mill and a lint mill were built in the town, driven by water so that they, too, were independent of taxed coal. One of his reported sayings is that the grandeur of the Solway was completed by the variety of vessels—often there were 40, 50 or even 60 at once in sight. However, he complained that the small ships which were all that could navigate the river to Dalbeattie suffered at the hands of the Customs house, as the fees were as high for a vessel of 50 tons as for one of 500 tons; and frequently there were delays until a Customs officer came to supervise the loading or unloading.

The various ways in which smuggling affected almost everyone living near or working on the sea is seen again in the life of Hugh Clapperton, the famous Dumfriesshire explorer. His biographer, R. D. Woodall, found that Clapperton went to sea as a cabin boy but, because he refused to accept authority, the Captain reported him for a petty act of smuggling at Liverpool. He was sentenced to serve in the Navy, where he distinguished himself so that he gained promotion which enabled him to retire on half pay to Lochnaben, where he planned his great African explorations.

Pitt's success in reducing smuggling was short-lived and most Members of Parliament had not time to learn the lesson that smuggling only prevailed when duties were high. As soon as George III needed money, firstly to pay debts left by the War of American Independence and secondly for the wars against Napoleon, parliament raised Customs and Excise duties which in turn increased smuggling profits—so that by the close of the eighteenth century tea duty accounted for 90 per cent of the price of the goods and the merchants' price was up to 15s per pound, wine duty was up to 11s per gallon, brandy to 22s per gallon and tobacco to 3s 2d per pound. Whisky duties had been reversed and now it was 10s 2d a gallon in England and only 6s 2d in Scotland—so once more it paid to smuggle it from Scotland to England.

Indeed, all these duties encouraged a huge increase in evasion, and for the next 40 years smuggling was probably one of the largest businesses in Britain. In 1825 the government published a list of all goods seized by the Customs men during the previous three years:

902,680 lbs of tobacco
3,000 lbs of snuff
19,000 lbs of tea
135,000 gallons of brandy
227,000 gallons of gin (Geneva)
10,500 gallons of whisky
42,000 yards of silk
2,100 Indian handkerchiefs
3,600 packs of playing cards
10,000 pieces of timber

By this time the smuggling of gin had been very much reduced from an estimated million gallons in 1795 to 227,000 gallons. Much of the free trade in gin was supplied by vessels from the Channel Islands, although mostly it originated from Dutch ports. Non duty-paid French brandy continued to be a problem, as it still is!

Rewards paid to seizing officers, listed in 1825, totalled £448,000, but some goods were destroyed and sales of seizures only brought in £282,000. Rewards for seizing goods were a continual bone of contention, foreshadowed by this short letter written by the collector of Customs in 1762:

> 'We beg leave to acquaint your Honours that on Saturday last, Captain Bell of the King's Cruiser here with a party of the Military employed by Mr David Douglas, Surveyor of the Customs brought up to the King's Warehouse here a seizure of 63 Ankers Foreign Brandy and Rum; the benefit of which was insisted on by Captain Thomas Bell for himself and his crew only. Mr Douglas at the same time insisted on being conjoined with them in the share and return of it. We enclose their several memorials on that occasion and wait Your Honours directions how we are to govern ourselves.'

The disputes are not surprising, as a single reward could equal six months' salary. Indeed, reading the reports one certainly feels that the Customs men often went to sea more in the hope of earning prize money than of serving king or government!

Robert Burns, Exciseman and Poet

Searching auld wives' barrels,
Ochone the day!
That clarty barm should stain my laurels;
But—what'll ye say?
These movin' things, ca'd wives and weans,
Wad move the very hearts o' stanes!
ROBERT BURNS (1759–1796) 'On being appointed to the Excise'

In the early years of the Napoleonic Wars the revenue service had a vacancy for an Exciseman which was filled by the appointment of the poet Robert Burns. He needed extra income to supplement his farming at Ellisland so friends procured for him this much sought-after job. Secretary Pearson issued the following order:

'To James Findlay, officer, Tarbolton. The Commissioners' order. That you instruct the bearer, Mr Robert Burns, in the art of gauging and practical dry gauging casks and utensils; and that you fit him for surveying victuallers, rectifiers, chandlers, tanners, tawers, maltsters, &c; and when he has kept books regularly for six weeks at least, and drawn true vouchers and abstracts therefrom (which books, vouchers and abstracts must be signed by your supervisor and yourself, as well as the said Mr Robert Burns), and sent to the Commissioners at his expense; and when he is furnished with proper instruments, and well instructed and qualified for an officer, then (and not before, at your perils) you and your supervisor are to certify the same to the Board, expressing particularly therein the date of this letter; and that the above Mr Robert Burns hath cleared his quarters, both for lodgings and diet; that he has actually paid each of you for his instructions and examination, and that he has sufficient at the time to purchase a horse for his business. Excise Office. I am your humble servant, A. PEARSON. Edinburgh, 31st March 1788.'

Having successfully completed his course of instruction Burns took up his post at Dumfries with a starting wage of £50 per annum, rising to £70 two years later and then to £90—but the officer had to provide his own horse. However, it proved to be a full-time job, covering 10 parishes, often involving rides of 200 miles in a week, leaving so little time for farming that he left his holding and moved into a house at the foot of what is now Bank Street in Dumfries. Although his service with the Excise was short, his widow was paid a pension of ultimately £12 a year until her death in 1834.

While on duty watching for ships Burns spent some time corresponding with a Mrs Dunlop. One letter, dated 'Annan Waterfoot, 22nd August 1792' concluded: 'So ends this heterogeneous letter, written at this wild place of the world, in the intervals of my labour discharging a vessel of rum from Antigua. RB.'

Mrs Dunlop lived in Ayrshire and was 25 years his senior. When he was slow in replying to her letters he usually tried to find some excuse. These two examples throw some light on an Exciseman's life. In one he blames his delay on: 'The hunting of smugglers once or twice a week', and at another time he writes: 'Amid all my hurry of business grinding the faces of the Publicans and Sinners on the merciless wheels of the Excise'.

There were, of course, many references to smuggling in the letters, among them a mention of the report, in August 1790, from the Dumfries supervisor of Excise to his superiors in Edinburgh that he had heard that the crew of the king's boat had been drinking with known smugglers in Annan while other smugglers were unloading a cargo nearby.

In that same year the Guernsey sloop *John and Mary* was seized off Annan by the king's ship commanded by one Captain Cook and 1,071 gallons of brandy plus quantities of rum, geneva, tobacco and tea were found on board. In addition to the seizure of the *John and Mary* it was reported that four other large cargoes, reported to be from Guernsey and Ostend with a total estimated value of over £7,000 had escaped seizure; as well as many other smaller cargoes which evaded the Customs cutters that summer.

In February 1792 a messenger informed Mr Findlater, supervisor at Dumfries, that a ship was about to make a landing of contraband goods near Annan. Burns, Crawford, Lewars, Penn and Rankin hastened to the scene where the *Rosamund* from Plymouth, a well-armed boat of around 90 tons, was found near Dornock unable to get off for want of water. The Excisemen were joined by a patrol of Dragoons from Annan, but they were only armed with pistols and were not strong enough to arrest the smugglers. Crawford galloped to Ecclefechan to fetch a troop of eight Dragoons and Lewars set off for Dumfries, returning after a long delay with 23 more Dragoons.

Burns was left in charge of his small force, with which he was impatient to attack; but it was not until reinforcements arrived, on 29 February, at low tide, that the attack took place. The ship's crew, some 20 armed men under the command of Captain Alexander Pattie, eventually fled across the Solway to England and Burns was left, with a troop of Dragoons, to guard the empty ship until she was refloated on a high tide. Before the ship could be refloated Robert Burns employed two carpenters for 11 days and four seamen for 9 days, at a cost to the Excise of £8 18s. The craft was finally taken to Kelton, on the Nith, for sale by the Collector of Excise; it was sold by auction for £186 in the coffee house at Dumfries in April.

The friendly rivalry between the Customs and the Excise sometimes became embittered by greed or the need for prize money; whereas the board of Excise and their local staff led by Burns might have been very pleased with their work on this occasion, the rage of the Collector of Customs knew no bounds. The *Rosamund* had first been sighted near Annan by Thomas Geddis, a Customs tidewatcher. He informed an Excise officer, and watched the vessel as she moved east up the entry of Sark, then went after it with the Excisemen to seize her but did not tell Dumfries when the smugglers escaped over the ford to Cumberland. The Collector reported to Edinburgh on 6 March 1792 that Geddis's negligence was due to the fact that he was covering for his fellow tidewatcher at Annan, an elderly man called Halliday who was in poor health. On 14 March the board replied, demanding Geddis's report so that his conduct could be considered. Unfortunately both the Collector's letter and Geddis's report are missing from the records. However, we do know that on 21 March the Board of Commissioners for Customs replied accepting the disagreeable fact that the Excise had seized much of the cargo that had been landed on the coast, but submitting that, as Geddis was the first person to discover the vessel and the first to communicate the information thereof to the Excise officers, whom he afterwards accompanied when they made a seizure of her, they considered that he was entitled to the 'informer's share' when the vessel was condemned.

To make matters worse the Collector of Customs had incurred

expenses of £2 4s 9d in going with a party of soldiers and a constable in fruitless search for the smuggled goods said to have been landed from the *Rosamund*!

While Robert Burns was keeping watch over the *Rosamund* and awaiting Lewars and the Dragoons he spent some of the time writing a poem in which he expressed his impatience; and a few days later he recited it to a company assembled at Provost Williamson's house, on the site of what is now 95 High Street, Annan. A plaque on the wall commemorates the writing of 'The De'il's Awa' Wi' the Exciseman'.

At this time Burns was reputed to carry a fine pair of double-barrel flintlock pistols with walnut stocks, made by Blair of London (these may still be seen at the Museum of Antiquities in Edinburgh). The most common weapons employed by smugglers were flintlock muskets and pistols, which used black gunpowder. The finest grains of powder were used for the pan whose flash primed the main charge inside the barrel. The Carsethorn Customs boat discovered how deadly such weapons were in 1789 when, attempting to seize a smuggling cutter, one of its crew was killed and another seriously wounded by a volley of shots from the smugglers.

It was said that Robert Burns was kind to the poor, probably as a result of having suffered poverty himself. An old local history records that he and his asistant paid a visit to the village the day before the annual fair. They approached the house of Jean Dunn, who was suspected of dealing in forbidden waters; seeing them coming Jean slipped out of a back door, leaving her servant and her own little girl in charge.

'Any brewing for the fair?' asked Burns.

'No,' replied the servant, 'we have no licence for that.'

'That is no' true,' said the innocent little girl; 'the muckle kist is fu' of the bottles of ale my mother brewed for the fair.'

'We are in a hurry just now,' said Burns, 'but when we have time we'll examine the muckle kist.'

Doubtless the chest would be empty by then!

Excisemen in general were looked on as enemies of the people and only the necessity of supporting his wife and children made Burns accept the job. On being appointed, one of his first letters was to the blind genius Dr Blacklock DD, who was born in Annan in 1721. He wrote:

Globe Inn — Noon — Wednesday

"Blessed is he that kindly doth
"The poor man's case considered" —

I have sought you over all the town, good Sir, to learn what you've done, or what can be done for poor Roabie Gordon. — The hour is at hand when I must assume the execrable office of Whipper-in to the blood-hounds of Justice, and must, must let loose the ravenous rage of the carrion sons of b-tches on poor Roabie. — I think you can do something to save the unfortunate Man, & I am sure if you can, you will. — I know that Benevolence is supreme in your bosom, & has the first voice in, & the last check on, all you do; but that insidious whore, Politics, may seduce the honest-eunlly, Attention; until the practicable moment of doing good is no more. —

I have the honor to be,

Sir, Your obliged humble servt
Robt Burns.

'But what do you think my trusty fier
I'm turned a gauger—peace be here.
I fear, I fear you'll now disdain me
Then my fifty pun will little gain me.
But I have a wife and two wee laddies,
They mun hae brose and brats o' duddies.'

However, Blacklock was understanding and they continued to be close friends, despite Burns's description of the ministers:

'Nay what are priests these seeming godly wisemen?
What are they pray but spiritual Excisemen!'

Allan Cunningham wrote in his life of Burns: 'To prevent the dis-
embarkation of run-goods, when smuggling craft made its appearance, was a duty to which the Poet was liable to be called, and many a
darksome hour he was compelled to keep watch, that the peasantry
might not have the pleasure of drinking tea or brandy duty free . . .
He was not a bustling gauger, nor did he love to put himself foremost
in adventures which he knew would end in distress to many.' And the
letter, written by Robbie Burns and reproduced on page 81, forever
proves his kindly heart.

Smuggling between Scotland and England

Aul' Johnnie was a pawky loon,
A pawky loon I trow was he;
At smuggling on the Solway coast,
Bune ithers aye he bore the gree.

Ilk creek and cove he weel did ken
Frae Airds roun' to the Hangit Man,
An' when a lugger was to meet
Aul' Johnnie sure was in the van.

Outwitted were the gaugers a',
Aul' Johnnie Girr was aye their match.
For ne'er wi' a' their plans sae sly,
The dodgin' smuggler did they catch.

SIR WALTER SCOTT (1771–1832), *Galloway Gleanings*

Among the many measures taken to stamp out smuggling between the two countries the duty on salt was equalised and the Customs and Excise departments were filled by ex-service Englishmen—or 'Southrons', as they were described in Scotland—who were accused of doing their best to demote all the Scottish supervisors. One of these Southrons was a Mr Pape, who was no doubt jealous of his subordinate, Joseph Train, the Annan supervisor, who had many friends in high places, including Sir Walter Scott. Train's downfall is described by John Patterson in his biography as follows.

'An opportunity soon presented itself to the ever-watchful Pape, a man who prided himself on the distress he could bring upon those who were under his sway. At Sark bridge Toll-Bar, near Gretna, there lived a person named Gibson who applied for an Excise Licence to sell spirits, which was refused. It appeared, however, that he had sold privately for the space of a month, without detection—a thing not at all to be wondered at, considering that the toll-bar was twenty-six miles from Dumfries. However, an eccentric individual, named German, commander of a preventive boat on the English establishment stationed on the Solway almost at Gibson's door, took a seat on the mail-coach that passed the smuggler's door about midnight and calling for a gill of spirits, easily obtained it, a sea-cloak which he wore disguising him from those who would otherwise have known him. This affair was represented in the worst possible light; and because Train had allowed a person of a different establishment to come into his district and make a detection which should have been made by himself, or some of his officers, he was reduced from the rank of Supervisor. At the expiration of six months he was however, on his own petition to the Board, restored to his former rank, and appointed to Castle Douglas District, vacant by the removal of Mr Porteous—another instance of petty tyranny of some of the Commissioners.'

While in the Castle Douglas district Train continued to send smuggling tales to his patron, Sir Walter Scott. The following extract and letter are reprinted from *Sir Walter Scott's Post Bag*, a selection from his letter books published by John Murray in 1932.

'Meanwhile, some of the old faithful have their reward. There is, for example, Joseph Train, the Exciseman: if he was as diligent in tracking smugglers as he was in searching for antiquarian lore, he well deserved Scott's efforts,—through Lord Liverpool and Sir Robert Peel—to get him promotion. A remarkable character discovered by Train was Myles Crowe, a smuggler, whose stories fill many letter-pages. Crowe, who has died not long since in Kirkcudbright, was a native of Galloway. He began as a teacher of English in the mountains of Man in 1771. He lived there for twenty years, and then returned to Kirkcudbright, where he became an agent for the distribution of contraband goods. Myles Crowe, writes Train, "actually believed in the existence of fairies, ghosts, and witches. I have often heard him tell a long story of a weaver who lived at a place called Cnok na Moar [*i.e.* the Fairy Hill], who from extreme poverty became rich by laying eggs like a Hen." It was Myles who told Train of the Manx custom in the seventeenth century, that if a man violated the chastity of a maid the Deemster gave her a rope, a sword, and a ring—with the choice that she could either hang, or behead, or marry the culprit. Train proceeds to relate that once when smuggling tea—then a precious commodity—Crowe poured a supply of it into his small-clothes. But he gave too long a stride from the quay to a boat; and the small-clothes, stretched by the wight of their burden, slit from side to side, the whole cargo of tea flowing into the sea. Finding the tea trade unsatisfactory, the smuggler went into the tobacco line; which resulted in this reminiscence, in Train's own words:

' "With a view of eluding most effectually the whole of the Revenue Gang, he rolled his person up from neck to heels, like an Egyptian Mummy, in Spun tobacco; and being a tall raw-boned gaunt person, he concealed nearly one hundred pounds weight in that way without increasing the bulk of his person to a size capable of raising the suspicion of the Revenue Officers, when he embarked at Pool-Vash for Kirkcudbright. Experienced smugglers generally roll the tobacco immediately over their under-garments; but Myles Crowe fell into the fatal mistake of placing the twist under them. But ere the vessel had put out to sea the tobacco threw him into a hectic fever which soon rose to such a height that he seemed to be In the very eve of passing from time to Eternity. Seeing him in such a deplorable situation, the sailors who came to his assistance, in the hope of permitting him to breathe more freely, opened the collar of his shirt, when unfortunately the tobacco appeared up to his very chin. The cause of his indisposition being thereby instantly discovered, the Skipper, in wrath at his vessel's being subjected to the risk of being seized at sea by such a paltry stratagem, immediately turned the unfortunate Crowe over to the officer on duty, who carried his seizure direct to the Custom House.'"

In 1820 an Act of Parliament was passed prohibiting the carrying of whisky from Scotland into England by land; it also provided that anyone carrying into or selling such spirits in England should forfeit 40 s for every gallon, or incur a penalty of £100. There were continual affrays between Customs officers and smugglers, and the preventive water guard boat belonging to the port of Carlisle was constantly busy watching the fords and the many rowing boats that crossed the estuaries of the Sark, the Esk and the Eden.

The only people permitted to carry whisky—and only a little at that—across the border without hindrance were the drovers, who went with their great herds of cattle from the Rood Fair at Dumfries to St Faith's Fair in Norfolk in November, where the East Anglian farmers bought store cattle to feed up for the London market. It seemed to be accepted by the local Excise that these men needed a wee drop to keep out the cold on their five-week journey.

James W. Brown in *Round Carlisle Cross* (published by Charles Thurnam and Sons Limited, who still maintain their good old fashioned personal service in their fine stationers' shop at 26 Lonsdale Street, Carlisle) highlights some stories of events:

'The obnoxious act had only been a short while in force before a regular business of smuggling was set on foot; and great ingenuity was shown in carrying it on. In little more than a year it was recorded that:

'"A great number of persons have lately been detected in smuggling Scotch whisky over the Border into England, and the Custom-house warehouse offers ample proof of their ingenuity. In order the more effectually to deceive the officers they get tin cases fabricated of various shapes and sizes; among those at the Custom-house we observe some in the form of knapsacks, cheese boxes, trunks, canteens, canisters, milk-cans, water-cans etc."

'Some of these were made "to fit the bodies of females," so as to give them what was euphemistically described as "a certain appearance", one of the receptacles holding four gallons; and others to imitate the portfolio of a distributor of number-publications. One man was detected with seven cases, holding about three pints each, in the pockets of a shooting jacket; all of which would seem to suggest a degree of simplicity on the part of the officers, who, however, are stated to have been "pretty well aware of these contrivances, and it is not easy to deceive them".'

Later an instance is given of the ingenuity or dexterity displayed by some of the smugglers for the purpose of evading the vigilance of the Excisemen.

'The following incident occured one day in the vicinity of Rockcliffe, Cumberland, which, for dexterity and good management, will perhaps bear comparison with any we have yet placed on record.

'A smuggler, returning from the North, laden with the "Dew of the Mountains", which he carried in bladders; and accompanied by his faithful dog, was pursuing an unfrequented path along the banks of the Eden leading towards this city, when the enemy, who had been on the look-out, suddenly made his appearance at a short distance. To save the whisky by flight was impossible; he therefore tied the bladders fast round the neck of the dog and sent him into the river. The canine culprit just entered the stream in time to evade the rage of his pursuer; he forded the river in safety and faithfully deposited the cargo on the opposite bank, where it was received by a "trusty brother of the trade", who had been waiting for that purpose.

'During the time the dog was crossing the river, the smuggler made his escape, leaving the Excisemen fairly outwitted.'

Another story of the Exciseman's experiences runs as follows:

'On Wednesday morning last (November 3rd 1824) as Mr Thomas Morpeth, Supervisor of Excise, was going between Longtown and Brampton attending the Collector, who was on his journey collecting the duties of Excise, he, being about one hundred yards before the Collector, came up to a man with a horse and cart, which he supposed to be laden with whisky, brought from Scotland; but not thinking it prudent then to search the cart, he waited for the arrival of the Collector and his attendants, who discovering that the cart was loaded with Scotch spirits, immediately seized the whole, gave the horse and cart into the charge of his two attendants, and arrested the man, whom he took along with him, in the chaise, to Brampton, where the horse and cart and 26 gallons of spirits, were safely deposited in the Excise office.

'On the following morning the man, Thomas Boys of Lochmaben, was committed to Carlisle Gaol, by Mr Ramsay, for want of bail.'

In the previous century the gaoler at Carlisle was hated by the Customs because so many smugglers held there had managed to escape.

A few days earlier than this, three Officers of Excise seized thirty gallons of smuggled whisky which had been buried in a dunghill near Floriston Bridge while the smugglers reconnoitred or took refreshment.

These stories collected by James Brown are shown to be even more remarkable when we realise that the fast-running tides made the fords at the head of the Solway which crossed Kirtle, Sark, Esk and Eden a dangerous journey even for legitimate travellers on horse and foot. On the south bank of the River Esk, opposite the fording place, was a little public house which in 1790 displayed this warning notice:

> *Gentlemen here take a guide,*
> *To either Scotch or English side,*
> *And have no cause to fear the tide.*

Many Scottish farmers risked the fords with a cart and horse to get a load of Cumberland coals for 1s 6d—coals shipped across would have cost 4s or 5s, and this at a time when many lived on a weekly wage of around 6s. The iniquitous tax on coal which had been transported across water continued until 1830 and was another vexatious duty which turned the ordinary people living around the coasts of Scotland against the government; and one which, incidentally, did not affect those on the English side of the Solway where coal was produced in large quantities. Coal at this time was relatively cheap where it was produced and consumed locally, but its price became prohibitive to all but the very rich when transport costs had to be paid and when a heavy duty was levied because at some stage it was 'water borne'. This duty bore particularly heavily on both agricultural and manufacturing projects in south west Scotland where at that time no coal was produced and wages of 1s 2d (6 new pence) per day (without food) for hedging or draining meant that peats were the only fuel which could be afforded.

The cross-border smuggling of spirits became so rife that lower duties to be levied at the distillery (the minimum still capacity to be eligible for a licence was reduced to 400 gallons) were introduced in April 1825. The duty on whisky was then 2s 3d per proof gallon. This measure encouraged the setting up of larger licensed distilleries and put out of business many thousands of small illicit stills hidden throughout the country—in 1797 no fewer than 859 stills were seized in Scotland. Several were in production within 10 miles of Annan but so well was their secret kept that the government could get no accurate count. A fine new distillery was built at Distillery Farm, Annan, and a large new brewery was built in what is now Delsanex Works in Port Street, Annan.

My grandfather recalled one of the last of the famous Annan smugglers, Morrice Bell, whose occupation was whispered with bated breath; he may even have been the hero of this tale of a border smuggler:

'On his way across the Border with several kegs in the bottom of a light cart, he was obliged to stop at a toll-bar somewhere near Gretna to awaken the keeper to let him through. While hailing this functionary, an Exciseman pounced upon him from behind the house and arrested the cart, kegs, smuggler and all. The horse's head was turned Annanwards, the Customs Officer, quite proud of himself, walking with the smuggler at the horse's head. But the toll-keeper grasping the whole situation, quietly slipped after them, and aided by the darkness as the cart rumbled on, he noiselessly removed a keg and laid it quietly down at the roadside. A second time, and even a third time he repeated this, the Exciseman and his prisoner little thinking of what was happening behind them.'

On reaching Annan a triumphant report was made to his superiors by the Exciseman, and his mortification can well be imagined when the cart was examined and found empty. One rather wonders what the smuggler thought of it all!

A great blow was struck at the smugglers in 1828 when the remaining rights of the Duke of Atholl in the Isle of Man were bought for almost half a million pounds, thus denying the use of Manx harbours for trans-shipment of foreign goods to local smugglers. It is almost unbelievable that it was only as recently as 1854 that Excise duties on spirits on both sides of the border were equalised and smuggling between Scotland and England finally came to an end. It was probably the coming of the railways which brought about this long overdue and very sensible decision, for honest rail passengers (some even Members of Parliament travelling to London) objected violently to being searched between Gretna and Carlisle for smuggled goods.

The notice exhibited by the railway companies warning would-be smugglers said:

The public is requested to take notice that the transmission of all foreign and colonial spirits from Scotland into England by land is contrary to law.

All Scotch spirits found in transit per the Caledonian or North British Railways, in less quantities than twenty gallons, and all such spirits of that or greater quantity, unaccompanied by the necessary permit are liable to be seized by the officers of the Excise.
All packages containing liquids of any description are liable to detention on suspicion.

As the railways grew in strength they had a revolutionary effect on the entire Solway sea trade. In 1853, after only 30 years' use, the Carlisle to Port Carlisle canal closed and a year later a railway opened in its place. Ships were getting bigger and trains faster so in 1857 the railway terminus was moved down the Solway to Silloth and regular sailings, helped by steam paddles, went to Liverpool, Douglas, Dublin, Belfast and the Scottish Solway harbours. For a number of years still the principal ships continued to call at Annan Waterfoot. In 1866 the wooden passenger and cargo paddler *Arabian* was used on the Annan and Dumfries service to connect with Silloth and sometimes went direct to the Isle of Man. Sailings to Liverpool were the last regular service from Annan but by 1869 the seagoing trade from harbours above Annan was so small that the Solway Junction Railway Coy was allowed to build the viaduct from Bowness on Solway to Seafield at Annan, thus cutting off the Sark, Esk, Eden and Port Carlisle from seaborne trade. Annan gained its second railway station and became the legitimate market town for several Cumberland parishes.

My great-grandfather attended the opening of the 2,000-yards-long trestle bridge. My grandfather recalled going to see the bridge the morning part of it was destroyed by blocks of ice in 1881. My father travelled in the guard's van of one of the last trains to cross the bridge, around 1922. And I walked on it, carefully avoiding the holes and the rustiest parts, a few weeks before it was demolished, in 1934.

Today the stone embankments at each end are all that remain of a mighty financial and engineering achievement that, sadly, was never a financial success, but nonetheless marked the end of an era—the smuggling era in the Solway Firth.

Returning to Honest Ways

Annan was then at its culminating point, a fine, bright, self confident little town.

THOMAS CARLYLE (1795–1881), *Reminiscences*

After 100 years of smuggling Annan began to gain some legitimate prosperity which, according to my grandfather, dated from around 1805. His conception of prosperity was backed by the greatest thinker and writer ever schooled in Annan, Thomas Carlyle, who always kept in touch with Annandale and each year sailed on the twice-weekly steamer from Liverpool, to land at Annan Waterfoot for a holiday among his own people at Scotsbrig Farm, Middlebie.

Graham Smith, Librarian of HM Customs and Excise, kindly drew to my attention a trip made by Carlyle in 1842 on the revenue cutter *Vigilant*, a vessel of some 100 tons. Carlyle described being rowed from Margate Pier out to the *Vigilant*, sailing to Ostend and back to London:

'It was a long swift Royal Navy kind of boat, the boat crew, six stalwart, clean washed silent men in little turned up straw hats with tarpaulin or waxcloth and the name *Vigilant* gilt-lettered on the brow of each.

'The cutter *Vigilant* is a smart little ship, rigged, fitted, kept and navigated in the highest style of English sea-craft; made every way for sailing fast that she may catch smugglers and frighten them from work on these shores. Outside and inside furniture, equipment, action and look she seemed a model; clean as a lady's work box; sea-worthy, work-worthy in all points whatsoever. Her jibsail of extraordinary magnitude a very field of canvas, was the main thing that struck you in all her rigging. We understand it was made of thin pliable cloth, so that in all degrees of wind, even the lightest degree it might be able to bag itself—and make itself available for motion.

'The crew consisted of some nineteen, all picked men. A Captain—Richard Gowland, in a blue-laced coat, in blue-laced cap and white trousers, an honest Lieutenant in similar trousers and blue spenser with a landsman hat. The Captain, a weather tanned but healthy firm little figure of five and forty, instantly struck you by his air of good natured energy, simplicity, intelligence and civility, a massive closed mouth, spontaneously not spasmodically closed, full of valour and benevolence, and a pair of large, sternly observant but affectionate almost mournful eyes, contributed to form a true Captain's face; to which the firm broad figure and modest simple carriage gave the best impression.'

He noted with interest the docking procedure at Ostend. The Captain's orders were given 'with brief emphasis without noise but with imperative decision, "Ease the main sheet, Down the Jibsail, Ashore a hawser, Check her".'

Carlyle confessed that to a landlubber like himself the whole paraphernalia of the vessel was fascinating and the language of the seamen most enlightening!

The return journey was direct to London, which gave Carlyle even longer to observe the cutter at work. While they were sailing up the Thames there was a sad mishap:

'The very steamers could hardly keep pace with us. Once in the brisk breeze there went off somewhere a kind of sudden screech; our enormous jib-sail of thin cloth had gone in a moment, close by the rope, swift as fate; torn to a single thread and trailing there in the water! The ship gave a little lurch, the Captain's eyes, a sudden twinkle, no other change observable: in ten minutes more they had the old sail gathered neatly for mending and a fresh jib flying as before. To see men so perfect in their craft, fit for their work and fitly ordered to it was a pleasure.'

It was by such chances of fortune that a revenue boat could lose a valuable prize.

I expect that the prosperity of Annan was based on the profitable effects of war on the local smuggling and farming industry, for certainly by 1810 plans had been drawn up to build the fine quay which still exists at the foot of Port Street. The Britannia Inn and the warehouses were built later along Port Street, fronting the dam or creek which was fed by the Mill Lade.

In 1819 the Hallmeadow Merse between the town of Annan and the Waterfoot was embanked at a cost of £3,000 by John Irving, Laird of Newbie, to make the river navigable up to the town for 300-ton vessels. The steamship proprietors built two piers at the Waterfoot and a public subscription of £640 provided a good road. My grandfather claimed that the Inn at the Waterfoot was then built by a man who had prospered in the smuggling trade.

Small ships and boats for all kinds of trades had been built at Annan for many years, but it was not until the start of the nineteenth century that the ships became progressively larger. John Nicholson and Company built some extremely fine ships on a site near the present slaughterhouse, on the edge of the merse. Then, however, the railways became all-important and the impressive nine-arched bridge was built at a short distance north of the great cotton mill chimney and straight through the site of the shipyard. Ships were then built on both sides of the Dam—the local name for the mill stream which used to feed the harbour but is now closed off—above the railway bridge.

The ships were launched almost broadside at the height of the big spring or autumn tides, and a most impressive sight it must have been as they rolled mightily before settling down on an even keel. The large ships were then taken to Liverpool to be fitted and rigged, after which they drew too much water ever to return to Annan. The largest of these ships was the 900-ton clipper *Elizabeth Nicholson*, launched in 1863; and the last was the *Sarah Nicholson*, launched in 1865. Both these ships were too large for the old building berth and Tom Willacy, harbourmaster for 38 years after the Second World War, believes that they were built on land between the town quay and Waterfoot Road; from there they could slide gracefully into the tide, encouraged no doubt by the cheers of several thousand spectators.

In the eighteenth and nineteenth centuries trading ships were owned in shares of one or more sixty-fourths and many Dumfriesshire and Galloway families held shares in one or more ships, such as the brigantine *Morton Castle*, 137 tons, and 87 feet long, which was built in Glencaple in 1857. Even at that late date the share included the boats, guns, ammunition, small arms and appurtenances. When I succeeded John Kendall and Son as auctioneers in the seaport town of Maryport I found that in the nineteenth century the firm had often sold one or more sixty-fourth shares in ships. These sales took place in the Coffee House in Senhouse Street at 6.30 in the evening. Records show disappointing results at one auction in May 1895, when one sixty-fourth share in the *Peter Iredale* received only one bid and was withdrawn from the sale; two sixty-fourth shares in the barque *Castle Holm* were bid to £45 each but withdrawn below the reserve; and a lot consisting of 18 £50 shares (£40 paid up) in the Maryport Steam Shipping Company were bid to only £2 16s, when they also failed to find a buyer.

When the Commercial Bank was founded in Scotland in 1810 and became one of the pioneers of branch banking, it established its sixth branch in Annan in 1812—surely a sign that the days of commercial prosperity had arrived. Earlier those astute members of the Dumfries and Galloway community who had made considerable profits from smuggling mistrusted banks, with good cause, for disaster had struck down all the local companies. The Dumfries Bank had a short life, from 1766 to 1772, when it was fairly insolvent but was taken over by Douglas Heron's Ayr Bank—which must also have been insolvent by that time. Douglas Heron's bank had offices in Dumfries and Ayr. Known generally as the Ayr Bank, it lasted from 1769 to 1773, when it had grown into a substantial and mismanaged business, which went bankrupt causing great losses to the businesses and people of south-west Scotland. The Dumfries Commercial Bank was set up at a prosperous time, in 1804, by James Gracie, with the assistance of his son and another partner; but by 1808 they were only able to pay their depositors half of what they were due. (They did, however, produce most attractive guinea notes, one of which I possess.)

The Annan Commercial Bank branch, however, prospered in times when not only were businessmen of enterprise growing wealthy but their workers had better wages which helped them save a little for a rainy day. No longer did they need to find a convenient hidey-hole for their nest eggs, for in 1810 Dr·Henry Duncan, the Minister at Ruthwell, established a Savings Bank which has become recognised as the parent bank and inspiration of the great savings movement which now covers the civilised world. It is a far cry from the deposits amounting to £151 at the end of the first year of operation to the £3 million held in Annan Savings Bank in 1985—the bank having been managed by Annan people for Annan people until that year when as its last governor I negotiated its union with the Royal Bank of Scotland, which had already taken over the Commercial Bank of Scotland.

After the Napoleonic Wars great efforts were made to abolish smuggling finally. In 1822 the preventive forces were reorganised to form the coastguard service and barracks for them were built at many places, including Southerness and Carsethorn. It is a relic of those days that coastguards still have strong powers of arrest. In 1833 the Scottish Customs and Excise were finally merged in a United Kingdom Board and from 1856 Customs officers were no longer allowed to carry arms.

The reorganisation did not have an immediate effect, as these reports show.

'In 1826 an inquiry into the Revenue of Ireland reported that either by force or by fraud huge quantities of American Tobacco still found its way into consumption. Much of it landed in South West Scotland, then it was moved by small boats to Ireland.

'At that time the duty on tobacco was reduced from 4/- to 3/- per lb., but the report produced evidence that tobacco was landed on the English coast from American ships docking in Holland at 1/8d per lb. and 4d per lb. was paid to the person who carried it from the landing place to the Merchant's depot in London.

'It was reported in 1835 that every two months a Belfast trader sailed to Holland and brought back 40,000 lbs of tobacco. He landed it disguised as barrels of herring with 100 lbs in each barrel. One load of 150 barrels cost the Revenue £3,000 in lost duty.'

However, the Customs men were not always outwitted. One of their most successful cutters was the *Castle Edwin*, stationed on the Cumberland coast, which is recorded in two fine paintings of 1822 by Robert Salmon. Newspaper cuttings attached to the reverse of the pictures tell a story:

'The morning of the engagement, the pilot cutter *Castle Edwin* fell in with and captured the *John and William*, a very shallow American smuggling schooner nearly sixty miles between Irishtown and Glenehad Head (coast of Ireland) with thirty three bales and a great quantity of manufactured tobacco estimated to be worth a great deal. The *John and William* was on her maiden voyage and her crew of eight men were all taken

'Hoisting sail off Carsethorn', by Michael Barton

with the first mate before they could get out the long boat and make their escape. This is the third capture made by the *Castle Edwin* within the past twelve months, beside engaging a lugger with her boats, which succeeded in escaping by a breeze springing up when the boats were within 1–2 mile of her.'

Nevertheless, by 1830 the total Customs income at Dumfries had fallen to £3,763; the staff had to be reduced, and the Customs Port of Kirkcudbright was amalgamated with Dumfries. It was a fairly prosperous time for Dumfriesshire and Kirkcudbrightshire, with harbours bustling with coastal traders. Foreign trade was scarce, however, and the joint Customs income in 1831 amounted to £5,089 only. It was a small return for so much effort; and the new railways opening up the remote parts of the country played a vital role in helping the Customs men to put an end to wholesale smuggling, for they made communication so much easier. The great free trade movement also played a vital role in putting the smugglers out of business, when its campaign to abolish Customs duties succeeded in 1842 in freeing several hundred imported articles from tax, reducing tax on others, and culminated in the repeal of the Corn Laws in 1846.

In 1832 the harbour at Dumfries was deserted when the sailors took their families and fled from the terrible cholera epidemic which killed 400 people and reduced the Customs staff to three: a collector, earning £300 pa; a comptroller earning £200 pa; and a searcher and coastwaiter on £100 pa. In 1870 the *Establishment Book* has the following record of the principal officers and their salaries:

DUMFRIES

Collector and Examining Officer. 200*l.*, to 250*l.*	James Millar (250*l.*, inc' to 300*l.*)
Clerk, 3rd Class, and Examining Officer. 30*l.* to 120*l.* (Also 30*l.* per ann. to cover travelling charges, &c. in visiting Glencaple and Carsethorn.)	William Muir
1 *Writer.* 5*s.* 6*d.* to 8*s.* 6*d.* a day.	
Outdoor Officer, and to act as Clerk. 59*l.* per ann.; and 1*s.* day pay, or 16*l.* per ann. in lieu thereof.	Nicol Macintyre
Principal Coast Officer at Kirkcudbright. 80*l.* per ann.	James McRobbie
Principal Coast Officer at Barlochan. 80*l.* per ann.	George Fotheringham

In 1833 this great anti-smuggling port came to the end of its exciting life. The Dumfries collection was discontinued and it became part of the Customs port of Ayr. Little did they think then, Customs men and smugglers both, that 150 years later the lonely bays of the Solway Firth would again be used for smuggling, not teas and silks but evil and destructive drugs—on two occasions in 1987 bales of cannabis were found on the Scottish Solway shore.

And a new dimension enters the battle, from the skies above, with aircraft and helicopters now used both by the ingenious and ruthless drug smugglers and by the ever-watchful Customs men.

Epilogue

When I rode my pony along the shore as a boy I wondered sometimes what happened to the smuggling leaders who became so well known to the Customs that they were an embarrassment to their well-to-do local trading friends. There are few records of any local heroes being executed; so, did they go away and buy a plantation in the colonies? Or did they obligingly retire to the Isle of Man? Or had they to be bribed or rewarded by their friends to leave the district peacably?

I have never found the answer; but once, when looking for something else, I discovered in *Morrison's Decisions* the report of a Court of Session case of 1757 which looked as if the town magistrates had helped a free trader to change his name and quietly go away by creating him a Burgess of Annan (although at the trial none came forward either to deny him or to admit his name before he earned his Annan Burgess Ticket).

It was in those days of considerable value to be a Burgess of a Royal Burgh, as the better-documented case of John Smith, Burgess of Annan, shows. The Guildry of Inverness had seized and confiscated goods landed by him at the harbour as having been imported contrary to the Acts of 1672 and 1690. It was pleaded for Smith that as a Burgess of Annan he was entitled to deal in foreign trade in any Burgh of the kingdom, and further that the goods had been bought in London and could not therefore by the article of the Treaty of Union be considered to be foreign goods. Against this the Guildry argued that though John Smith indeed had a Burgess Ticket from Annan he seemed never to have paid Scot and Lot there, neither did he have a residence or carry on any trade in Annan; therefore, said the Guildry, his Ticket gave him no right to any privileges in another part of which he had not the freedom. Nevertheless, the decision of the court was that goods brought from London were not to be regarded as foreign goods and the Guildry were liable to John Smith for the value of the goods confiscated—and also for damages and expenses.

APPENDIX 1

DUMFRIES ESTABLISHMENT—COLLECTORS OF CUSTOMS

1710		William Edgar
1710		John McDowell
1717		Walter Murray
1719		James Young
1720	23 May	John Crawford
		Received £11 per annum rent for providing Customs House until 1728 when Maxwell found a more convenient place.
1725	12 November	George Maxwell
1742	29 April	John Young
1759	1 June	David Blair
1771		Robert Maxwell, dismissed 1778
1779	15 March	Willwood Maxwell, superseded Dec. 1780
1780	12 December	David Staig
1813	21 October	John Staig
1843	7 December	William Tennant
1845	26 December	Alexander Rose MacLeay
1850	22 March	James Lawson
1852	12 June	Edward Waters
1854	6 February	George Gwyther
1857	26 February	James Millar
1876	24 March	Alexander Scott
1880	7 January	Daniel Dunglinson

EIGHTEENTH CENTURY DUTIES

Customs Duties were levied on the following goods as well as many others which bore duty at a very low rate and were not smuggled commercially:

Books	Sugar
Coal	Tea
Silks	Tobacco
Spirits	Wines
Sails	

Excise Duties were levied on the following goods as well as many others:

Beer	Notepaper
Candles	Playing cards
Glass	Printed cottons and silks
Hops	Soap
Leather, Hides and Skins	Salt
Malt	Spirits produced in Britain

Returns for 1796

For some strange reason there was also a duty on auctioneers, which in 1796 totalled $110,483; but owing to the honesty of auctioneers it was the cheapest duty to collect, the cost being only £900 in one year.

In the same year the salt duty was £7 per cwt and yielded a net revenue of £454,000.

The total year's receipts were as follows:

	GROSS	EXPENSES	NET (After costs and drawbacks)
Customs	£6,381,902	£391,000	£4,533,400
Excise	£10,960,425	£504,000	£9,155,500

They provided much the largest source of government income and included the following from Scotland:

	GROSS	EXPENSES	NET
Customs	£248,537	£120,182	£128,354
Excise	£419,500		

The De'il's awa wi' the Exciseman

The De'il cam fiddling thro' the town,
And danced awa wi' the Exciseman;
And ilka wife cries 'Auld Mahoun,
We wish you luck o' your prize, man.'

We'll mak our malt, and brew our drink,
We'll dance, and sing, and rejoice, man;
And mony thanks to the muckle black De'il
That danced awa wi' the Exciseman.

There's threesome reels, and foursome reels,
There's hornpipes and strathspeys, man;
But the aye best dance e'er cam to our land,
Was—the De'il's awa wi' the Exciseman.

ROBERT BURNS